THE PYROMANIAC IMAGES

Theory-fiction of generative AI

Pierre Cassou-Noguès & Gwenola Wagon

SET MARGINS, 2026

CHAPTER 1

Augmented Realty

Max and Norma were quite convinced that one of the greatest problems in human life was figuring out how to dwell. They even believed that they had read, in the works of certain philosophers, like Heidegger that dwelling was the problem of human life. Not only dwelling somewhere, in the sense of finding a place to live, but also just dwelling – full stop.

Dwelling, that is, establishing relationships of coexistence that suit one's environment. Obviously when you say that, you haven't said anything.

Who and what do these relationships of coexistence suit? The people doing the dwelling, or the environment in which they dwell? What, then, is the environment? Other humans with their own social relationships, flora and fauna, stones, wetlands, cities? Does the Earth itself, as a separate entity, belong to the environment? All places have a history, like an unconscious, and of course, in order to inhabit, it is important to know that history, to adapt to it, to take a stance on it without necessarily conforming to it. And the future? Do we need to think about the future or dwell in the present?

And what does it mean to **coexist**? Living, all the forms of life we can imagine – do they not all imply coexistence with an other, with an outside that constitutes its environment? Then why should some forms of coexistence be privileged over others?

These are questions Max and Norma would have been unable to answer. They would have refused to mention "the Good" or "the Beautiful", "harmony" or even "durability", in order to associate dwelling with a "good" or "beautiful" or "harmonious" or even "durable" coexistence.

They would have also refused to reduce the problem of dwelling to the difficulty of dwelling somewhere. It would be perfectly possible, they thought, to inhabit a territory – a great plain or a big city or a coastline – without ever settling down somewhere, drifting around instead like nomads. By defending nomadism, Max and Norma were a little naive, a little Deleuzian, and very much in "bad faith". During the first quarter of the 21st century, the area was facing both a housing crisis and an environmental crisis; dwelling was a problem in both senses of the word: dwelling tout court, as well as finding a place to dwell.

So, Max and Norma opened a real estate agency.

We could say that they hadn't understood anything from Heidegger, or Deleuze and Guattari. They were more on Le Corbusier's side, *mutatis mutandis*, changing what must be changed.

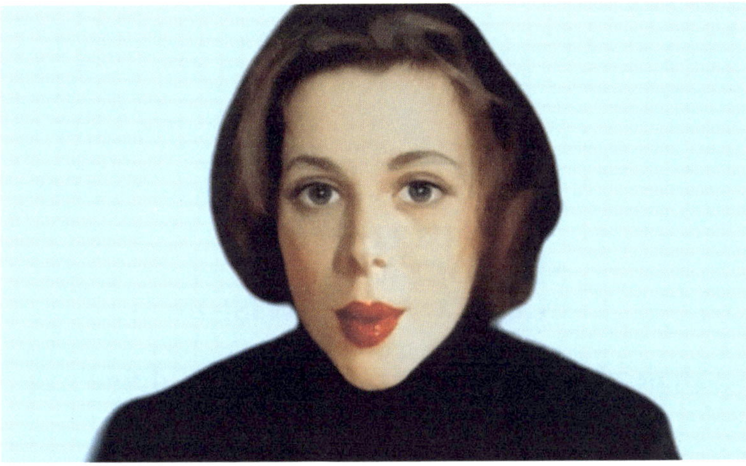

**EXCLUSIVE!
SEMI-DETACHED HOUSE
IN YELLOW SUBDIVISION**

Made entirely of concrete, this semi-detached house is an extraordinary example of Brutalist architecture.

Its stripped-down lines and robust structure will ensure that it lasts forever.

Located in a quiet neighborhood, this property has the perfect atmosphere for anyone looking for an oasis of calm and a tranquil environment.

PEACEFUL AND BRIGHT
MAGNIFICENT ART DECO VILLA

This extraordinary villa is perfectly situated in a highly sought-after neighborhood. It boasts vast living spaces, a large tree-filled garden, and a pool. Despite unfortunate damage from a recent fire, this property has huge potential. The high ceilings, solid wood doors, stained glass windows, and original molding are all waiting for you to restore them to their former glory.

Design and architecture lovers will jump at this unique opportunity to own the house of their dreams. Inspections have been carried out to ensure that the structure of the residence meets security standards.

We sometimes act as if one fine day artificial intelligence fell from the sky, ready to transform a natural landscape. But we must remember that it has a prehistory, and that the landscape was by no means natural. It was already "post".

In various fields of study, landscapes were dubbed "post-industrial", "post-tourism", or "postmodern". Above all, the term postmodern applied to cities or architectural ensembles.

However, the importance of "post" was mostly ensured by the fact that a growing number of users, and in particular post-tourists, were no longer looking at landscapes except through the screens of their phones. They were taking pictures; they were filming. Sometimes, they wouldn't post anything on social media; they would just compare the images that were beneath their eyes, on the phone screen, to posts. It was about seeing reality as a post. Well before AI, in the era of social media, a way of seeing had developed, or a way of not seeing: a way of thinking of reality as a post on a social network, of making reality a post that was just waiting for the network that would suit it.

Post-ure is the attitude that consists of confusing reality with the post we make it into on social media. We can also talk about post-reality to designate this abstracted reality, a reality reduced to a post or set of posts.

Post-ure was very important in Max and Norma's chosen profession. The agent's art is in steering their client toward this post-ure in order to make them see the house as a post, and forget the underlying reality.

Sometimes reality resists its own reduction to posts: you can hear the noise of trains passing outside the windows (in the photographs, drawn curtains hide the tracks); you can see an enormous water stain from a pipe explosion. Maybe the space just has a certain melancholic quality which was absent in the beautifully-colored images.

The real estate agency was called Augmented Realty. Under this name (which, incidentally, Norma was quite proud of herself for inventing), Norma had created a social media account. In the form of a grid were all the houses that Augmented Realty had ever sold or put up for sale, and even a few extra ones. Max and Norma would lie here and there, as real estate agents often do.

Their lies did not only have to do with post-ure, but also betrayed an interest in or temptation for fiction, which developed afterwards.

Geographically speaking, the agency set up shop in a resort town on the Atlantic coast. In the years preceding the Catastrophes, business was booming. Although everybody knew that the region was under particular threat from the environmental crisis, the houses on the coast were attaining astronomical prices. This was probably a form of denial, a way of saying "it won't happen", even though everybody knew that it was going to happen.

Lying, denial, post-ure, fiction – the era was marked by several forms of reality avoidance.

With Augmented Realty, in any case, Max and Norma were living on the coast and living well. Their own housing is not important. They lived, by proxy, in the houses they were selling. Sometimes they even lived in them physically; they would settle down for a while. That's why sometimes you can see them in the photographs – in the kitchen or sitting in the office.

Most of the time, Norma would take pictures of the houses and Max would write copy for the ads. But they often exchanged roles.

The ads, like the photographs, were guided by the implicit but strict rules of their profession. In the bedrooms, the photographs had to be taken from the corners, from a perspective that would make the space look bigger. For the kitchens, the colorimetry of the images would be systematically modified to obtain the kinds of acid hues that whet the appetite. The swimming pools were photographed from the second floor and subtly enlarged on a specialized software.

Likewise, the ad copy was composed of ready-made expressions: "wood floor, molding, fireplaces", "historic charm, modern comfort", "great potential: a few renovations are to be expected"; "this enchanting home is sure to pique your interest". Max was considering publishing a kind of glossary that would inventory all the expressions used in the ads – the most common and the most rare – alongside guidelines for their usage. This glossary would allow ads to be written in the same way that brain-teasers are solved. You would look up all the expressions that could match an old three-room unit, and try to fit as many of them as possible into a single 500-character ad.

Sometimes clients would buy a unit without even visiting it, either because they lived too far away (Augmented Realty sold a lot of second homes) or because the clients were only post-uring.

And sometimes the same clients, disappointed in the unit they had bought, would spend their time sitting on the couch, immersed in their phones or busy watching television.

So before AI, screens had become the most fundamental and intimate machines for living in. Augmented Realty's clients would settle into their homes through the mediation of screens. If Le Corbusier described houses as **machines for living in**, screens were machines for living in the machines for living in.

GREAT DEAL. MOVE QUICKLY

In the heart of an unpleasant neighborhood, we offer you a small, dark apartment located on the ground floor of a dilapidated building. The unit contains a single room that serves as living room, bedroom, and kitchen. The entryway has been fitted with a toilet area.

A narrow, treacherous staircase allows you to reach the basement, which would be difficult to finish and is home to a number of pests. The neighborhood is hard to reach by public transit. There are not many shops around.

FILTERS AND METAFILTERS

A **filter** is a coherent deformation of reality. On social media, filters allow images to be conferred a certain tone, by modifying their colors or adding shooting stars or rainbows to their landscapes. So it's about imposing a style, an emotion, or a context onto the content: sepia, like a '20s photograph, or a feeling of enchantment from the touch of a still visible magic wand. Other filters are applied to the face, to transform the user into a '50s actress, a kitten, an old man with a beard, or to make them look very happy or extremely sad or much older or much younger. These filters deform the image coherently, not randomly; they modify its tone – the tone of the colors or, more widely, the emotional or contextual tone of the image.

The expression **'coherent deformation'** comes from Merleau-Ponty, who uses it to describe the style of the painter and to analyze perception.[1] The philosopher argues that the painter, who has a recognizable style, produces a coherent deformation of reality. This deformation of reality, which is visible in the painting, then demonstrates the workings of perception itself, which seems to carry out a similar operation. Our various perceptions would resemble many deformations of reality, distinguishable from one another while still relating to the same object, like two paintings of the same chair by Picasso and Matisse. Ultimately, for Merleau-Ponty reality is nothing other than the system of its coherent deformations.

Social media did not invent filters, then, but rather multiplied them and made their usage easier and freer. Painters cannot really choose their style. The development of a certain style requires years of work, an amount of time whose cost is difficult to estimate. On the other hand, with a single click the user can bestow upon the dreary

1 Maurice Merleau-Ponty, *La Prose du monde* (Gallimard, 1992).

gray sunset outside the window of their apartment the warmth of an ad for a tropical island where you drink cocktails under swaying palm trees. And the cost and price of this filter can be easily measured.

The simple fact of taking a picture of the sunset and posting it on social media is enough to transform it, give it a "special something". That particular evening becomes integrated into the grid, the storyboard of a life lived like a film. There will be "likes", hearts, thumbs up. The social network, or, more broadly, the digital device, does not only make a multitude of filters possible, but itself acts as an original and fundamental filter. The digital device is a **metafilter**.

Filters and the metafilter produce post-reality. Post-ure entails ignoring the reality beneath the metafilter or confusing it with the post produced by the filters and the metafilter, thus forcefully pulling reality over the post. You can adopt the smile, the makeup, or the facial expression that the filter gives you, or you can ask a surgeon to subject your body to the filter's aesthetic.

ARE REAL ARTISTS REAL ESTATE AGENTS?

It's a question, as is the inverse: are real estate agents real artists? Through their work, artists create filters in a broad sense, in the sense of a coherent deformation. In so doing they give a certain shape to coexistence. They create devices of coexistence, not in the way that engineers and architects invent machines for moving across land, through air, or on water, for communicating, or for living on the coast, in the city, or somewhere either too hot or too cold. Artistic devices are ways of seeing, or, more than seeing, feeling, situating oneself, being part of an environment: they are both filters and devices for coexistence. That is how artists contribute to making our environments habitable. Real estate agents are in the same position. They don't build houses either. They are satisfied with renting or selling them, and, in order to do this, they develop certain ways of seeing. The so-called Airbnb style, a product of the first years of the 21st century, is a decorative as well as a representational style (with a slightly overexposed kind of photography).

What differentiates artists and writers from real estate agents is not that real estate agents are attached to commerce while artists and writers are liberated; they're all part of an economic context that is not necessarily the context of the market.

The real difference is that real estate agents are focused on housing. It is only in terms of housing that the real estate agent, in its current form, shapes coexistence. The housing crisis, the fact that 21st century society does not produce enough housing to house all its members, has given housing an all-consuming importance, and given the real estate market an absurd economic significance.

Yet housing is just one machine for coexisting among a multitude of others. In a well-functioning society, real estate agents represent nothing but one category of artists among others, just as in other periods there were painters of the fleet or ceramicists whose art only dealt with one sector of coexistence. It could well be said that artists, or writers, are agents (in the same way that realtors are agents) so long as they intervene in our coexistence and mediate it by offering it new possibilities, but this assertion requires that these agents be detached from the real estate function, or that that function be generalized. Artists and writers are agents whose work consists of expanding forms of coexistence.

The environmental crisis, the Catastrophes it has brought, reshuffled the cards (or should it be the files) for Augmented Realty. Reality no longer allowed itself to be confined in filters. It was spilling out. It was causing water damage that the agents could no longer hide. The pine forests surrounding the coastal resort had been decimated by droughts. The small city had flooded more than once.

The flood map, which was easily available on the internet, showed that a large section of the housing developments and the commercial zone would flood multiple days out of the year for a decade or two. After that they would flood at every high tide. Clients were hesitant to invest. The agency was in decline.

Norma was usually the one to retouch the housing photos. She would cover up the water stains on the walls or remove clouds of smoke from the sky. One day, when the supermarket flooded, she made the building look like it was raised on stilts. It would be accessible by boat; the commercial zone acquired a Venetian charm. Augmented Realty was responsible for a house across the street. It sold immediately.

This experiment gave the agents a lot to think about. They understood that they had to switch professions. Not only did Artificial Intelligence need to come to Augmented Realty's aid, it needed to replace it.

From then on, the agents only sold Artificial Realty. They were used to adding a few dream homes to the grid of available properties. It was a question of developing and systematizing this business of fantasy.

> *"It is out of a deep sense of compassion and for the highest humanitarian reasons that this chemical hoax has been perpetrated, this camouflage, this bedecking of reality in plumage it does not possess..."*[2]

In Stanislaw Lem's novel *The Futurological Congress*, this camouflage is achieved by psychochemical substances, pills that, when swallowed, affect the brain in a highly precise and localized manner. You see a garden instead of a traffic jam; you drink chablis instead of stagnant water. Psychochemical substances come to correct all the defects of a deficient environment. They take weary human silhouettes and give them strapping physiques and smiling, laughing, serenely exuberant features. They even allow the weather to be adjusted, or, in a kind of meticulous dissociation, permit you to speak to yourself as if you were speaking to another person.

Social media filters, which add magical colors to dark landscapes or replace unattractive pouts with starry smiles, have exactly the same function. They undertake a psycho-non-chemical operation. As has already been shown, their secondary effect is often a kind of schizophrenia.[3]

2 Stanislaw Lem, *The Futurological Congress* (Harvest Books, 1985), 102.

3 Anne Alombert, *Schizophrénie numérique* (Allia, 2023).

The psychoanalyst Carl Gustav Jung insists on the multiplicity that constitutes the human psyche. We contain various characters inside us which must be allowed expression to maintain the equilibrium of our psyche. Inside us there is always a man as well as a woman and other obscure non-gendered beings; there are also characters that exceed us, entering us into contexts larger than our own lives. These are archetypes, which determine our lives by making us play out old myths or ancient stories.

Social media filters seem to be the realization of Jungian psychology, but in a form that the psychoanalyst certainly never imagined. All of the characters that the user might express appear on a grid. The user can try them on one by one. In turns, he or she becomes a woman, or, for example, a cat. Or else the filter affixes an emotion to the face with such force that the gender showing through no longer matters. Sorrow, which deforms the user's features, is made incarnate on that face; that personified emotion, which in itself has no gender, is now the only visible thing.

Some filters suit the user better than others. These are added to 'favorites' so that they are always close at hand. Through them, the user expresses themself more easily and more happily. This is an exchange: the filter reveals something about the user, who is in fact a '50s actress or a cat or Sorrow, and inversely, the user lends the archetype the material of their body, so that the archetype can carry on with or further complexify its life.

On social media, these archetypes are not taken from legends, myths, or literature like the ones Jung was referring to. They are born and evolve through a complex selection process. Developers propose new filters for the platform, most are dead in the water, but some are adopted by users and taken over by others in higher and higher numbers, moving up the grid, gaining in popularity and visibility until other developers catch hold of them to modify them, refine their features, make Sorrow more sorrowful, and produce a new generation that will undergo the same process. More efficient than the time it takes for Jung's myths to be established, this selection process seems to succeed in isolating what the users (or a certain number of them) have in common, and crystallizing those features into a single character. Filters have allowed for the formation of true archetypes.

AI has transformed the real estate profession. It's no longer just a question of applying the Airbnb style like a filter on a phone. Agents are creating properties in parallel worlds, distinct from reality like dreams or fantasies, but a bit more solid, a bit more material.

Fantasizers. In stores, they try on clothing from Dior or Chanel just to see what it looks like. They test-drive sports cars during "open houses" organized by car manufacturers. And they visit luxury villas which they are entirely aware they can't afford, but for the length of the tour they settle in anyway, in a kind of waking dream assisted by that ritual with the agent showing them the utilities and the double parking.

But since the Catastrophes, the fantasizers have multiplied. We have all become fantasizers. And Artificial Realty, the Artificial Realtor, is directed toward them, toward us.

When AI makes mistakes, or when something bizarre appears in its writing or images, we sometimes say it's hallucinating. However, this trade in imaginary homes to which the agents have devoted themselves is not madness, but a systematic way to fantasize.

The clients know perfectly well, when they browse the ads on the website, or even when, on occasion, they make a purchase, that the properties do not exist. They let themselves be carried off on a waking dream, what could be called a fantasy. Reality is not exactly denied. The reality principle intervenes to dissociate the plane of reality from the plane of fantasy, but once this dissociation has taken place, the content of the fantasy can be shaped in a certain independence. Then reality stops bothering the realtor and the client, who can buy and sell a 5000 m^2 villa with an ocean view that will not be affected by floods or forest fires or tides of plastic.

That's what matters: keeping the Crisis at a distance. The clients rarely ask for the most luxurious villas. Because, ultimately, we rarely fantasize about winning the Olympic Games or becoming President. In most of our fantasies, satisfaction is obtained in a convoluted way, in the very limitation of the impulse, through perversion. Real estate fantasies are as perverse as sexual fantasies. The clients request: a fire-damaged villa, a yellow semi-detached house, a slumlord, a family home in disarray...

Nostalgia likely also plays a part in this.

As Alban Leveau-Vallier has demonstrated, AI is a "floating signifier".[4] The tasks that come under artificial intelligence's competency change with time, with the development of algorithms. In fact, artificial intelligence seems to bring together everything that's new, hard to get, and, in some way, profound. In the 2000s, algorithms programmed for playing chess came under AI's purview, whereas today AI is usually associated with image generation or the famous Large Language Models, or LLMs. AI is also increasingly mentioned in the realm of automated surveillance, as cameras become capable of identifying certain faces or situations. Social media filters use the same mechanisms: to transform a face, the algorithm must locate the same points (cheeks, chin, eyes) that automated surveillance locates when identifying a person. However, the expression "AI" is more frequently associated with facial recognition than with the use of social media filters.

In contemporary vocabulary, one might want to identify AI with algorithms that fall under the principle of "deep learning". But this definition, aside from the fact that it neglects local variations, could only fit into the contemporary context (the last twenty years) and could not take into account different kinds of algorithms, or mechanisms, that the expression AI could have designated since its appearance in 1953 as a research program opposing Norbert Wiener's cybernetics.

It would be better to accept the "floating" element that Leveau-Vallier ascribes to AI. AI designates whatever research promises us must happen.

4 Alban Leveau-Vallier, *IA. L'intuition et la création à l'épreuve des algorithmes* (Champ Vallon, 2023), 45.

Contemporary technologies produce new images and a new relationship between images and reality. But how do we define this new class of images, and at what moment and based on what criteria does the demarcating rupture occur?

Contemporary technologies are particular in that they produce images by transforming preexisting images. In contrast, the invention and development of photography produced new images on the basis of reality. Photography is a technology that is applied to reality to produce images. But this is not the case with contemporary technologies; rather, this is not what makes them novel.

AI, like filters, or the found footage of desktop films, are different modalities of a transformation of already existing images. AI image generation is based on learning that categorizes the images stored on the Internet and, in short, entails recombining abstracted elements from preexisting images. This logic of decomposition/recomposition is found to a lesser extent in a multitude of images, in photomontages, in the artist's process, as well as in conspiracy theory videos that dismantle and reassemble visual content found on the Internet to make it mean something else. Filters, which add a smile to a face or plant a rainbow in a landscape, also represent different transformations of an image which is, in itself, commonplace – so commonplace that it seems to preexist itself even when filmed in real time.

In *The Language of New Media*, Lev Manovich argues that one characteristic of digital media is that images lend themselves to multiple **montage.**[5] In the era of analog images, montage required costly tools and arduous work, while today you can edit a film on your cellphone. Montage was also mostly temporal, with sequences

5 Lev Manovich, *The Language of New Media* (MIT Press, 2002).

cut and pasted coming one after the other, whereas digital images made possible a smooth montage within the shot. The dinosaurs of *Jurassic Park* are blended with the decor where the actors evolve. With AI, this characteristic must be generalized. Not only do digital images allow themselves to be made into videos or exhibited in photomontages, they also lend themselves to multiple operations that do not involve solely cutting and pasting, that even go beyond retouching, and that take on unexpected and unpredictable logics. In the examples that Lev Manovich take, montage within the shot implies a few images which you can always recognize: the dinosaurs, the decors, the actors. The AI-image is produced from a huge quantity of images on which the algorithm has been trained. It is a new sort of montage within the shot which involves not a few images, not a thousand but more than we can count. The result is that we can no longer recognize the elements coming for the initial set of images. It is no longer montage. It is something else. Images now lend themselves to **manipulations**, of which montage is but one possibility.

In contrast to photography, contemporary technologies are particular in that they produce new images through the manipulation of existing images, rather than by being applied directly to reality. The images are manipulated – not just cut and pasted, but deformed, recolored, decomposed into abstract elements that might be recombined to display something other than their originally intended object, something other than the reality toward which they were meant to open. Manipulated images open two possibilities according to which they aim to replace reality or to be superimposed on it: madness or fantasy.

Max and Norma wanted to invest in an Artificial Intelligence villa, but they couldn't come to an agreement. Norma wanted a '60s villa that would remind her of the New Wave, while Max was stuck on the year 1927 and the Bauhaus.

So, the two styles must be melded together. It's a classic problem, and there is more than one way to proceed. Chronologically, the villa could be given a '60s wing and a '20s wing, gliding between the '30s, '40s, and '50s to connect the two wings. Or – though this is more risky – a blend could be attempted. With the blend function, you ask the machine to merge two (or three, or four, or five) images you have given it. The machine picks up new images from the intermediary zone between the initial images in its latent space. What will a blend between '20s architecture and '60s architecture look like? Will the resulting villa even be habitable? The human mind can not predict blends, it doesn't contain the same latent space as the machine.

The waterside villa in which Max and Norma physically lived at the beginning of the 21st century had to be abandoned. The two agents now live in a gray tower a few kilometers from the salt marshes which replaced their old neighborhood. They never go back, although, clearly visible at low tide, there still remain the villa's foundations, the kitchen floor tile, the square pit of the swimming pool. In the tower, their neighbors, who they sometimes bump into on the landing, who were already their neighbors during the time of the villas, are convinced that the coastal zone to which they themselves will never return is now being used for techno-biological experiments. They showed Max and Norma videos. They are living in madness while Max and Norma are living in fantasy.

Where do Max and Norma dwell? Fantasy does not build houses, it does not even help Max and Norma live in the tower which, in contrast, seems gray, rudimentary, and uncomfortable. Really, they don't live anywhere. AI has substituted itself for Augmented Realty, but has not really replaced it. The agents no longer facilitate residence or coexistence. Artificial intelligence has transformed them.

CHAPTER 2

Anarchives

The dunes rarely remain in the same state: their summit rises or falls; they meet or move apart. New valleys form and others fill, and all of these changes – or, this disorder – are the effect of winds which seem to use them at leisure. [...] This immense surface, akin to that of a raging sea whose tall stormy waves have suddenly been tamed, offers to the eyes only a blinding whiteness, a monotonous perspective, a naked and monstrous terrain; then, finally, a terrifying desert.

– Nicolas Brémontier, 1786[6]

The slightest wind carries the finest sands and blinds you [...]. The manner by which those highest dunes metamorphosize into valleys and mountains is quite singular [...]. The wind, being violent, bears the sand that forms mountains and fills valleys, at times even raising mountains to an extraordinary height, and where the mountain once was there forms a valley, revealing houses and trees formerly covered by those sands.

– Claude Masse, 1702[7]

6 Nicolas Brémontier, *Mémoire sur les dunes* (1786), cited by Joseph Bert, *Note sur les dunes de Gascogne* (Imprimerie nationale, 1900), 5.

7 Cited in Yannis Suire, *La Côte et les marais du Bas-Poitou vers 1700. Cartes et mémoires de Claude Masse* (CVRH, 2011), 10.

The sands that covered the church [...] continue advancing toward the east. There are times when this church appears exposed, but new sands, continually deposited by the sea onto the coast and heaped into mountains by impetuous winds, cover it once again [...] Now there is visible only an arid, deserted country covered with dunes, even in the town itself, and from which the foundations of houses and windmills sometimes emerge.

—Abbot Jacques Baurein, 1785[8]

When the western wind is somewhat violent, the sea causes even the hair of the boldest to stand on end, for it forms waves that create a terrible noise and that appear almost as high as the dunes; the sea appears white, and only with great effort is it possible to hear one's neighbor speak. And the vessels are helpless, having the misfortune of being close to the coast in such weather, the winds lifting them so impetuously that, falling back on the usually firm sand, composed, in many areas, of hard gravel, those vessels floating above shatter in an instant like glass. The coast is covered with the debris of such vessels that have, in different seasons, washed ashore.

—Claude Masse, 1702[9]

8 Jacques Baurein, *Variétés bordeloises* (Labottière, 1785).

9 Cited in Jean-Yves Blot's *Le Naufrage des Portugais* (Chandeigne, 2000), 70.

The rains that stagnate here in the winter, and the ardor of a sun entirely unobstructed by shade in the summer, seem to have condemned this plain to an eternal sterility. [...] The hills and the sandy high plains that form the surface of the Landes will remain in the future what they have always been since the retreat of the sea waters: sorrowful deserts, hideous places of solitude, sands burning in the summer, marshes and chasms in the winter—a ruinous country in all seasons.

—Guillaume Desbiey, 1778[10]

10 Guillaume Desbiey, *Trois mémoires d'un précurseur landais méconnu* (SHAAPB, 1991), 7.

It is from this lofted belvedere that the eye may admire the superb Basin of Arcachon [...]. At your feet, limpid water moves gently and rhythmically, struck with regular strokes by the fisherman's large oar.

—Jacques Arago, 1829[11]

Added to the sweetness and steadiness of its climate is the quite local influence of air impregnated with resinous emanations spread round by the forest's pine trees. A stay in the countryside is thus eminently favorable to those with weak chests and delicate temperaments, women and children, people with lymphatic conditions, and all who, tired of the big city, [...] are in need of calm, rest, and invigorating, pure air.

—Oscar Dejean, 1845[12]

11 Jacques Arago, *Promenades historiques, philosophiques et pittoresques dans le département de la Gironde* (Suwerinck, 1829), 26.

12 Oscar Dejean, *Guide du voyageur à La Teste et aux alentours du Bassin d'Arcachon* (Chaumas, 1845), 152-153.

That distinct scent of seawater, the scent of those resinous woods that surround the Basin; the appearance of that basin that reflects, by darkening, the bright azure of the sky; those porpoises approaching from the high seas with the rising tide, somersaulting, at every moment, so pleasantly atop the waves; everything, all these new sensations that I feel, makes this little voyage delightful for me.

— Anonymous, 1825[13]

The villas built on the edge of the beach reflect coquettishly in the calm, limpid water of the Basin; the others, seated delightfully in the forest, are surrounded by age-old pines and evergreen strawberry trees: all under the influence of the saline evaporations of the sea combined with the balsamic emanation of the forest, each possessing unique flowers, foliage, and shade.

— Oscar Dejean, 1858[14]

13 Anonymous, "Une saison chez Legallais", published in *Bulletin de la SHAAPB*, n°76-77, 48.

14 Oscar Dejean, *Arcachon et ses environs* (Chaumas, 1858), 127.

It's a true country home, a palace that unites all the amenities procured by fortune: order, good taste, and cleanliness transported to an uncivilized country. A peristyle, with pilasters of the kind that adorn almost all the homes of India's wealthy colonists, joins the two lateral wings. It is under that graceful peristyle, exposed to the refreshing northerly breeze, that one finds the bathers' rooms.

—Jacques Arago, 1829[15]

A colonial Eden with the sea, the mountains, the forest. [...] We row, we sleep, we roll in the sand, we wander naked across the landscapes of Texas. I did not know that such a strange, beautiful land existed where it was possible to enjoy oneself at home, with none of the sailor's *malaise*. On the ocean dunes, there is no "trace" of our era – one believes oneself to be living the first ages of the world. I run; I face the great green waves, roll around, dry myself in the sand, and gather shells for my collection.

—Jean Cocteau, 1917-1918[16]

15 Arago, *Promenades historiques...*, 27.

16 Jean Cocteau, *Lettres à sa mère* (Gallimard, 1989), 420.

They come here only with the idea of living "in the meantime." This precariousness places them in a condition like that of a house builder; they quite simply, quite straight-forwardly make themselves a lodging, a shelter—nothing more. They undertake a project that is pure and unencumbered by pretensions of history, culture, and contemporary taste, using the humble materials they find nearby. They do this with their hands.

—Le Corbusier, 1929[17]

The city barely exists. It is almost dissolved. With the little resistance it offers to reality, this is not surprising. But it is almost terrifying. No one seems to be playing with the little cubes, the little houses, the little casino. A toy with no child-master: there is nothing more solitary, nothing sadder.

—Hélène Cixous, 1986[18]

We will soon spend the afternoon on the beach, returning to Paris in one hour, enough time for a swim. Our descendants [...] will descend by helicopter straight into the water, surfacing to dry themselves on board during the return trip.

—Paul Morand, 1960[19]

17 Le Corbusier, *Une maison, un palais* (Crès, 1928), 48.
18 Hélène Cixous, *La Bataille d'Arcachon* (Trois, 1986), 12.
19 Paul Morand, *Bains de mer* (1960) (Arléa, 1990), 139.

Marine erosion is mainly due to a shortage of sand on the coasts. This phenomenon, caused at the end of the postglacial transgression, has been accentuated in contemporary times by human actions [...]. The expected rise in sea level, generated by global warming, is likely aggravating this erosion. It translates to an inland shift of the boundary between marine and continental domains. This retreat of the coastlines, often accompanied by the destruction of coastal equipment and buildings, is accelerated by severe storms.

— Anonymous, 2023[20]

Sea level rise is unavoidable for centuries to millennia due to continuing deep ocean warming and ice sheet melt, and sea levels will remain elevated for thousands of years. Global mean sea level rise will continue in the 21st century. [...] Due to relative sea level rise, extreme sea level events that occurred once per century in the recent past are projected to occur at least annually at more than half of all tide gauge locations by 2100 and risks for coastal ecosystems, people and infrastructure will continue to increase beyond 2100.

— Intergovernmental Panel on Climate Change, 2023[21]

20 "Document d'information communal sur les risques majeurs de la ville de La Teste de Buch", 8.

21 IPCC, "Climate Change 2023: Synthesis Report", 77.

CHAPTER 3

Pyropictomaria

THE SPECTACLE OF ENERGY CONSUMPTION

The purpose – the use value – of things produced by humans is ultimately found in the pleasure they provide. Their cost and exchange value derive from the energy consumed during their production. We can think of a society as a tool for transforming the energy stored in the Planet, provided by the Sun, wind, and tides into human pleasure. To warm oneself by a fire, or to admire the spectacle of a flaming forest, is to establish the most direct relationship between energy and pleasure. The image of a forest on fire adds the mediation of the image to the relationship between energy and pleasure, and allows the expenditure of energy to sustain this pleasure long after it ought to have dissipated.

The spectacle of fire has not always offered the best ratio between the amount of energy and the amount of pleasure. In the past, before the Catastrophes, for many people a car ride would have yielded a better return – less energy consumption, and possibly greater pleasure. The NASCAR races on TV were, however, already founded on the pyropictomaniac principle. The objective was to provide pleasure to the viewer through the spectacle of energy consumption. From home, in front of a screen, the viewer could observe images of an astounding use of energy. It was like a forest fire mediated by both cars and the image itself, with this double mediation's function being to increase the yield between energy and pleasure.

This is also true of catastrophe films, a beloved Hollywood genre since the studios' beginnings. These films plots revolve around a catastrophe, whether of the natural sort (tornados, hurricanes, floods, earthquakes, droughts, dust storms) or provoked by humans, or even aliens. Compared to the spectacle itself, these differences ultimately matter very little. This cinematographic genre was probably the first to popularize the spectacle of energy. Among the many gigantic

blazes from famous films, let us cite a few examples: *In Old Chicago, Gone with the Wind, The Towering Inferno, Bambi, The Day the Earth Caught Fire, Fahrenheit 451, The Sacrifice, Days of Heaven, Keeper of the Flame, Backdraft, Ladder 49...*

Pyropictomania is the habit of taking pleasure from an image that makes the consumption of energy visible with no other aim than to provide that pleasure. The incendiary images that internet users collect today, the NASCAR broadcasts of the past, and the aforementioned catastrophe films all have to do with pyropictomania. This is also the case for AI-generated images. AI-images are the result of an energy consumption intended for human pleasure, and they present themselves as such. Energy is consumed in the process of making the image provoke pleasure. The image, which portrays itself as an AI-image, makes a spectacle out of this energy consumption.[22] Every internet user who generates AI-images (even if these images have a practical, definite purpose) is a pyropictomaniac, whether they know it or not. These images can certainly represent something other than a fire, such as a dwelling, an animal, or a landscape—as long as they are recognizable as AI-images, they also **show** the energy consumption that produced them.

The content of the image, like the façade of a dream, returns energy consumption to a latent state. It is also a mediation intended to improve the output of the image, that is, the relationship between energy and pleasure.

Today, however, the majority of pyropictomaniacs have reached a level of consciousness that renders these mediations—which, to them,

22 With her idea that contemporary images depend on a thermodynamic paradigm that has replaced the optic paradigm associated with photography, Hito Steyerl proposes a different approach to this same problem. Hito Steyerl and Noa Levin, “Hot Takes: Image Production in Times of Climate Crisis, Noa Levin in Conversation with Hito Steyerl”, *Foam, All About Photography* 66 (May 2024).

seem to interfere with the energy-pleasure relationship – useless. They now only look at images of fires.

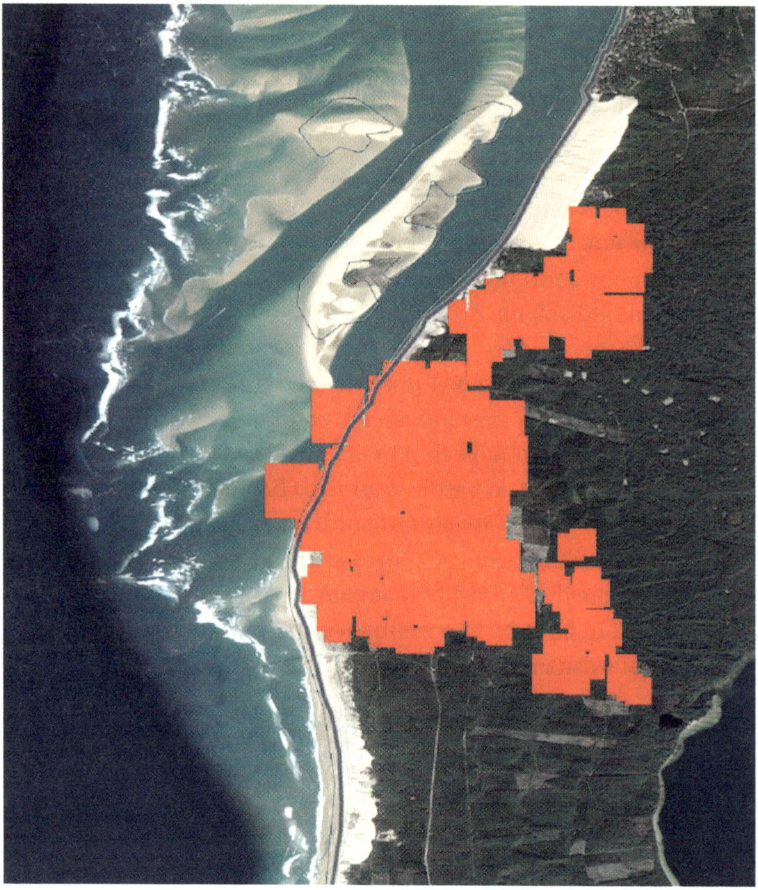

The first images began to circulate during the great forest fires that marked the beginning of the Catastrophes. From their front yards and their cars, people took pictures of the fires striking near their homes; firefighters took pictures from their trucks; all were posted on social media. The firefighters' videos were particularly spectacular, giving the viewer on the other side of the screen the impression of being inside the fire. All were witness to great skies with mounting pillars of smoke, vermillion sunsets, dark clouds hiding the sun, and immense curtains of flame rising above and engulfing houses, trees, and roads.

Fires are "hyperobjects" that are impossible to view globally, in their entirety.[23] The fire-images are pixels in a vast, twinkling constellation that must be coordinated or resynchronized to adequately represent the intensity of the fire. They perfectly illustrate the "synhaptic" mode of surveillance that was established in cities.[24] While satellite views and maps do exist, they offer only abstract and slightly shadowy images.

We can offer all kinds of hypotheses as to why certain users began posting incendiary images and others began looking at them. Some certainly wanted to bear witness; others simply wished to stay informed. There were filter and meta-filter effects. Uploading such images to the internet and passing them to the other side of the screen contributed to a certain "derealization" of reality, or even to the creation of another, more easily assimilated reality. The smoke that rendered the air unbreathable was reproduced on-screen as a

23 Timothy Morton, *Hyperobjects: Philosophy and Ecology after the End of the World* (University of Minnesota Press, 2013).

24 Pierre Cassou-Noguès, *La Bienveillance des machines* (Seuil, 2022).

glorious sunset one might dream of seeing on an exotic island. The flames devouring a family's home and entire property became a universal and distant catastrophe – like the ones we are so used to seeing on screen – rather than an intimate tragedy.

All of these ideas are acceptable, though it must also be acknowledged that, from that moment on, the viewer watching those firefighters' videos began to feel a new pleasure at the sight of nature offering its most precious belonging: time.

Quand tu pars en
vacances...

Mais qu'il y a une petite
odeur de brûlé

HUMAN TIME, NON-HUMAN TIME, AND VALUE

A commodity, like a coat, has a use value. The coat's purpose is to keep us warm; it has quite a high use value depending on the weather. But commodities also have exchange values that allow them to be traded. Let's say we exchange a coat for some apples: how many apples for that coat? In Marxist theory, the exchange value of a commodity is determined by the time necessary to produce it; its value is derived from time. The value of the jacket thus depends on the time spent to manufacture it compared to that needed to harvest the apples. How many apples could have been harvested in the time needed to make one coat?

Money, which soon intervenes to mediate these exchanges, ultimately represents time concentrated into commodities. Producing a coat requires planting cotton or flax, harvesting, transporting, and weaving it, then cutting and sewing the resulting fabric. It takes time, time that gives the coat its value.

Marx was right, save one mistake: in determining value he only accounts for human time, the amount of time that humans spend planting, harvesting, weaving, sewing, etc. The time that passes between sowing and harvest, which humans might spend doing something else, is, for Marx, a sort of nothingness, a neutral area that can be erased in our calculation of the coat's value. Non-human time—the time the flax needs to grow, or the time it takes to accumulate the energy to transport the fabric—doesn't count. For non-humans like plants, the sun, or sheep (if the coat is made of wool), time seems to pass pointlessly or, at the very least, to not possess the incompressible nature of human time. It is as if it could be stretched or condensed to the point of self-annihilation. But it is not true. It is exactly the opposite that proved to be the case.

In the era of pyropictomania, human time no longer has value. It is infinitely available. Humans are unoccupied. Just as we once imagined remote islands where we could live off the berries and roots growing around in abundance, the automation of production often allows the population to be fed and maintained, in at least minimal comfort, with just a few hours of work. The majority of humans don't work at all.

On the other hand, energy involves non-human work that takes time – the time of the sun, the trees, the wind, the tides, and even the machines. The flax that makes up the coat can still be recycled and turned into a shirt or skirt, while most of the energy used in production has already been irreversibly used up. This is time, non-human time, that has been lost.

For the pyropictomaniacs, the **value** of a commodity derives from the energy, or from the non-human time, that its production requires.

Until recently, the energy at humans' disposal came from the sun and filtered through plants. Plants would gather energy from the sun and store it in a form that humans could use: in food (energy stored in plants released inside the human body) or in external combustion (energy released as heat or transformed into movement through the intermediary of a machine).[25] The use of other energy sources was still marginal. There were a few mills and windmills, but they only performed secondary work. Humans depended on plants that alone could capture and transform solar energy. This energy could filter through other forms of life before being absorbed by humans, who would eat animals that had, themselves, eaten plants. It could also be transformed through chemical processes. It was in this way – by energy storage in plants and then by chemical transformations – that coal and oil were formed, with which humans then fed machines.

The situation has changed since the machines themselves became capable of storing energy. Energy now has two different sources. It can be obtained by nuclear fission. This produces a large amount of energy almost instantly but can only take place inside power plants that have a short life span and take a long time to build. Nuclear energy therefore assumes a labor time on the part of machines that, as of now, does not seem possible to reduce. On the other hand, machines can replace plants to capture solar energy (as well as energy from the wind, tides, or the earth's internal heat). The capture and transformation of this energy is slow and requires work on behalf of the sun, wind, or tide.

25 Pierre Cassou-Noguès, Stéphane Degoutin, and Gwenola Wagon, *Welcome to Erewhon* (Web Series, Irrévérence Films, 2019), chapter Humans-Plants.

In both cases, the accumulation of energy requires non-human time. In the current state of technology, it is that time that cannot be reduced; it is that time that defines the value of commodities.

Back when human time seemed to be the only determiner of value, humans largely drew on the energy that had accumulated in plants since their first appearance on the Planet. We can say that they appropriated the energy stocked in the Earth or extorted the Planet for its labor time.[26] The incendiary images would represent a new extortion, if the pyropictomaniacs did not consider them a gift from the Planet – an offering, for pure, unmediated human pleasure, of its accumulated energy.

26 Jason W. Moore, *Capitalism in the Web of Life* (Verso, 2015), Introduction and Chapter 5.

IMAGES ARE NOT COMMODITIES

A particularity of **information** is that it can be abstracted from its initial format and converted into another. More specifically, it can be duplicated. The letters we write on paper can be read aloud, and that same message, that same information that appears on the paper, can then be recorded in analog form on a wax disk, or in digital form in a data center. The message, first encoded in writing and materialized on paper, passes through another, sonic form, consisting of vibrations in the surrounding air, and ends up coded in the depth of the groove on the disk or a series of 0s and 1s, open or closed switches. The letters can also be copied, and now there are two paper copies of the same message.

These same considerations apply to images. In principle, any image, as long as it contains some kind of message or information, can be reproduced. However, the cost of reproduction could be quite high before images started being coded digitally, as sequences of 0s and 1s. Digital images are very easy to reproduce. They can be displayed on a great number of screens.

Images are not like other commodities. A coat has a cost—the non-human time needed to manufacture it. Making a second coat will cost about the same. Of course, this is not entirely true if the first coat is a prototype and the second marks the beginning of a serial production. The production of the second and third and fourth coats, however, requires a comparable amount of energy and similar material processes. On the other hand, the production and reproduction of an image involve completely different processes. The image is a photograph of a fire. A hectare of pine trees burned down so that this image could exist, whereas all you need to do to reproduce the image is copy the sequence of 0s and 1s that code it. That cost is almost nothing compared to the cost of production.

We can imagine an exchange of commodities, or a trade in which each commodity has a value corresponding to its energy expenditure. The price of a coat compared to that of a pound of apples would be strictly proportional to their energy cost. Images cannot be integrated into this trade of commodities, for their cost is not derived from the production of the copies to which the user has access. In one way or another, the cost of manufacturing the image must be distributed across its reproductions which, in themselves, cost nothing.

In another society, the subject of an economy of images might be entirely secondary.

It costs almost nothing to reproduce an image; producing it may have a cost equivalent to tons of apples, dozens of coats. The official doctrine among the pyropictomaniacs is that the cost of producing an image is social, and must be shared among all members of a community, who then have the right to enjoy reproduced copies of the image. The internet is free, the majority of images are open-access. Were there any NASCAR races, they would be broadcast for free. However, forest fires are all that remain to entertain viewers and internet users.

The image producer is indirectly compensated by the state. Since everyone is capable of taking incendiary images, the pyropictomaniacs receive a universal salary that allows them to live in relative comfort. The production of material commodities is, for the most part, automated. Society does not need to encourage productive work. Human time no longer has significant value.

DF2R

Human time no longer has significant value, yes, but we must provide some nuance. **ABT** maintains its value. By **Available Brain Time**, we mean those moments when human minds, hypnotized by the images they observe, become more easily influenced.

ABT is generally used to increase the desirability and, by extent, the value of a commodity. For example, we witness a firefighter taking a swig from a bottle of soda in front of a fire. In an instant, that soda bottle becomes desirable, and this desirability is a quality of the soda just like its nutrition or taste – it increases its value. We can think of ABT like a tool that increases the value of the commodity. The value of these available brains, the cost of their production, must be included in the value of the commodity just as with other machines necessary for production.

ABT can also accrue its own value and be sold separately to businesses, humans, anyone who wishes to influence an election (for example).

The value taken on by ABT does not contradict the devalorization of human time. ABT is not human time in the Marxist sense. It is possible to listen to the radio or watch videos – thus making your brain available – while doing another activity, such as working, playing sports, walking, spending time with friends, etc.

ABT is secreted by the human body under certain conditions, but must not be confused with the labor time that, in Marxist theory, determines value. The cost and value of ABT depends on how difficult it is to create the conditions under which a human body produces ABT. We could compare the production of ABT in the human body to that of blood. Various methods have been developed to increase the daily production of blood in a human body. The production of blood takes time, but that time is not quite human.

In fact, the value of ABT, as with blood, is determined by the energy cost of its production: the human only comes into play to the extent that they contribute to the process's energy consumption. And, in the case of ABT, most of the energy is not consumed by humans, but in the production of incendiary images. Incendiary images possess an intense, hypnotic power; they increase the availability of the brain, but their energy cost is significant.

If the image producer is a professional who has set fire to a forest they owned in order to produce an incendiary video, they will certainly be compensated, according to the real value of the images, by the social networks, or the few television channels that stockpile the ABT. In other words, the image producer will be able to sell their images at the energy cost of their production. The most beautiful incendiary images, however, are often made by anonymous users who happened to be passing by on the road, or even by firefighters. These amateur photographers rarely get the opportunity to be compensated according to the value of their images. They certainly benefit from the universal salary, but when they post the images on social networks, most of the value is extorted from them.

As Samuel Butler has shown, we can think of machines as a fourth "kingdom", along with the plant, animal, and human kingdoms.[27] In Butler's thinking, each kingdom – plants, animals, humans, machines – is distinguished by a certain manner of expanding. Machines, more specifically, expand without having life, instinct, intelligence (in the literal sense), or consciousness. To search for life, instinct, intelligence, or consciousness in machines would be to believe that plants require the mobility of animals to evolve, or that animals require human intelligence. The fact is that plants evolve differently from animals, and machines evolve differently from humans, animals, and plants. We must therefore not attribute human or animal features to machines, but rather recognize their tendency towards a new kind of expansion.

In the age of pyropictomaniacs, machines are set to replace plants in the capture and storage of energy. Most of the plants still needed to feed humans and their domestic animals are grown by machines. They grow in large lamp-lit sheds powered by external solar panels. This new kind of agriculture has proved more efficient than the previous one.

Pyropictomaniacs may unconsciously believe that they no longer need the forests, or the energy storage that plants provide. Or perhaps it is out of nostalgia that they ask the plant kingdom to offer them, just one last time, and for no goal other than pure pleasure, that stored energy.

It is difficult to enter into the psychology of pyropictomaniacs and to understand what they seek, and what pleasure they find, in this spectacle of energy consumption.

27 Samuel Butler, *Erewhon* (Trübner and Ballantyne, 1872).

Butler's thinking does, however, shed light on an associated phenomenon. Provocative or shocking images have always played an important role in the development of social media. Since the dawn of the Catastrophes, new users signed up to see images of the fires devastating forests across the Planet. Yet, in the capitalist system of the pyropictomaniacs, social networks belonged to a few shareholders who accumulated colossal fortunes. One can say that the shareholders used these machines to enrich themselves. But, taking on Butler's perspective, we can also say that the machines used this desire for enrichment, or for the capitalist system, to expand.

What's important is that the value of the last stocks of energy accumulated by the plant kingdom was transferred to social networks in the form of incendiary images, where it was then used to produce ABT. From the point of view of value transfers, pyropictomania converted energy stored in forests into images, and converted the images into Available Brain Time. The energy, converted into heat, made it possible to produce a quantity of ABT of immense value, which the machines themselves or the networks' shareholders (depending on the perspective one adopts here) then found at their disposal. We can say that machines extorted this value, and this ABT, from the plant kingdom.

As ecosystems became impoverished, a new profession emerged: searching social networks for rare images of the first fires. Some images, even those posted by anonymous users, had already circulated widely and informed the gaze of pyropictomaniacs. For example, in a short video, a user whose identity has not yet been determined films a van on fire in a pine forest in the middle of summer. He is perfectly aware that he is witnessing the start of a megafire but posts the video on the network without taking the trouble to call the firefighters. This video has acquired the same significance among pyropictomaniacs as the film *Arrival of a Train at La Ciotat* did in a previous era. It is the birth of a new art of the image.

However, in contrast to those worn-out images, pyromaniac historians, like treasure hunters, scour the social networks for images that have only received a few hits. At the time of the first fires, thousands of users posted their videos at the same time. Some went unnoticed and remained so because they were poorly captioned either by the users themselves, who did not type the right keywords or chose a thumbnail unrelated to the content of the video, or by AI that may have been confused by these unprecedented images.

The search for rare images generally involves working on keywords. The researcher trains a search engine by directing the algorithm towards a certain type of incendiary image and then imagining the combination of keywords that will move it closer to the sought-after image. They include place names, names of people, and thematic variations: #fires #Palisades #lostcat... Like a spell performed in a magical ritual, words invoke images, with the difference that the researcher must always dream up a new spell that will reawaken the flames of the past.

A man films an accidental fire and posts the video on the platform.

These images can take on immense value. If the value of a thing is in the energy required to produce it, images that have not been seen or reproduced are real treasures.

They contain within themselves all the value of a forest, as yet unscathed by reproduction. The videos are most often sold at auction without having been viewed, but rather on the basis of a few screenshots and the reputation of the researcher who unearthed them. The purchaser sometimes makes them available to all users of a social network, where they then produce ABT; but most often they keep them in a personal collection, either for their own pleasure or for that of a small community who can then witness the spectacle of energy consumed for itself alone, in a direct relationship to the Planet.

Most of the incendiary images are generated by AI. Since the forests have regressed so much, there was no other solution to satisfy the pyropictomaniacs' taste. But if AI-image generation began as a last resort, it aroused a particular craze, then a real addiction, and finally an artistic movement that could be described as neo-romanticism.

As has been said, AI image generation is generally representative of unconscious pyropictomania. The user can assign any content to the image – maybe it will show an animal, a home, or a landscape rather than a fire. This content comes between the consumption of energy and the viewer's gaze. It masks the reality of the process, which consists of wasting energy for a certain human pleasure, or jouissance.

On the contrary, pyropictomaniac art, insofar as it is self-aware, is the mise en abyme of this process and of the relationship between the Planet and humans that this process engages. By generating incendiary images, AI simultaneously mediates the relationship between nature and humans, represents it as an image, and reproduces it as a process. It mediates the relationship by interposing itself between the spectator and the forests that have burned, and whose incendiary images have nourished it when it was trained; it represents the relationship by capturing it in an image; it reproduces the relationship by consuming energy in order to make that image.

For all these reasons, AI recalls the "mind's eye" invoked by romantic artists such as William Blake or Caspar David Friedrich, and contrasted with the actual eye. Indeed, AI is not about flatly imitating nature as it appears to the actual eye. The cloud of smoke generated by AI may very well not take the spiraling, intricate form that a scientist would deem accurate. The AI-image, which itself emerges from a process comparable to fire, has a deeper relationship with the

Planet than one of mere resemblance. AI, which combs through all human images to find some sort of essence, would therefore represent, to paraphrase a famous formula by Friedrich, no longer what the artist "has in front of him, but what he sees inside himself."[28]

These parallels arise all the more readily as Romantic art, in its themes, appears today as anticipatorily pyropictomaniac.

28 William Vaughan, *Friedrich* (Phaidon, 2004), 68.

Specialists are generally able to distinguish between photographs and AI-images. This difference can determine the value of the image, and it counts much more for collectors than for simple amateurs who do not completely disavow AI-images. AI produces roughly similar images, but what matters is not so much this resemblance as the internal relationship the image has to the Planet, due to the fact that the image itself depends on the energy consumption that it also portrays.

The generation of AI-images and the search for rare images in the dark corners of the internet both require new uses of language. These two kinds of images can be found in the same place, on the screen or what we once called the "desktop", and are invoked in the same way through a certain linguistic play. Those who seek old images and those who try to create new ones must both type words on a screen. They are not the same words. And in neither case are they the words that would describe the image in a purely human use of language. Alongside the usual and purely human use of language, these two methods of working with images are each linked to a specific poetic art.

The paradox is that if words produce the visible, that visible escapes them. The visible thus created is not framed by what is sayable. The fire, the cloud of smoke, the consumption of energy, remain indescribable, and we could say that they detach themselves from the language that is nevertheless at their origin. This is a process closer to the invocation of ghosts in spiritualist rituals than to description: words give rise to apparitions that surpass them.

How can we describe the clouds of smoke that form in the machine when they respect neither physics nor the typologies invented by meteorologists? How can we describe a cloud that we recognize as a cloud but that does not fit into any known classification, that has none of the recurring characteristics by which we distinguish different kinds of clouds? AI clouds and the forest fires above which they rise illustrate a new sublime that goes beyond the human mind and language. This new sublime seems to be integrated into a process that stretches from the Planet to the screen-machines in which the human figures only for a moment.

By blending or prompting, almost all inhabitants practice image generation. They spend their time, which no longer has any value, watching and creating virtual fires that they then circulate on social networks.

This form of pyropictomania can be considered an addiction. It threatens to replace all digital addictions: online shopping, cute animals, memes, rocket accidents, dating apps, pornography, and competitive sports – which were only manifestations of disguised, repressed, and unconscious pyropictomania – have almost entirely disappeared from screens. Pyropictomaniacs quickly finish their online shopping before returning to their platforms of choice, where grids of flames undulate ad infinitum.

The addiction seems to stem from the indefinite nature of the game and the element of chance that presides over it. Pyropictomaniacs enter words into the machine in the same way that old gamblers used to insert coins. They wait a few moments. This delay is an important element of addiction; it is the period of time that gives us the old adage, "the die is cast." The ball spins in the roulette wheel, the reels of the slot machine roll, the images begin to appear, blurry, before the user's eyes.

Dozens of seconds pass. Finally, the result: four images are displayed on the screen. The platforms have continued to produce images in sets of four, arranged in a line or in a 2×2 grid. The effect of this number on addiction is difficult to determine. The images depend on the prompts given, the user's skills in that poetic art, and also a bit of chance: the machine draws randomly from the area of its latent space determined by the user's linguistic prompts.

Image generation is thus a game of language, chance, and patience. It seems to take up and link together different features from earlier games, crosswords for linguistic skill or sudokus for the art of combination, lotteries and casino games for chance, card games for patience...

The gain, for the pyropictomaniac gambler, lies in the aesthetic characteristics of the images. Neither money nor any purely physical appetite come into play. The gambler seeks only the sublime. This is probably why image generation is superior to the old games and has been able to supplant them: a relationship with the Planet is established, which offers the player, again and again, the spectacle of energy stored in time and now utterly wasted.

CHAPTER 4

The Blending Diaries
Norma's Notebook

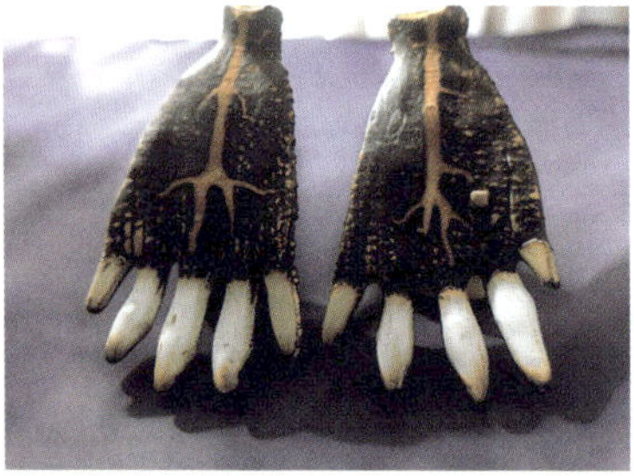
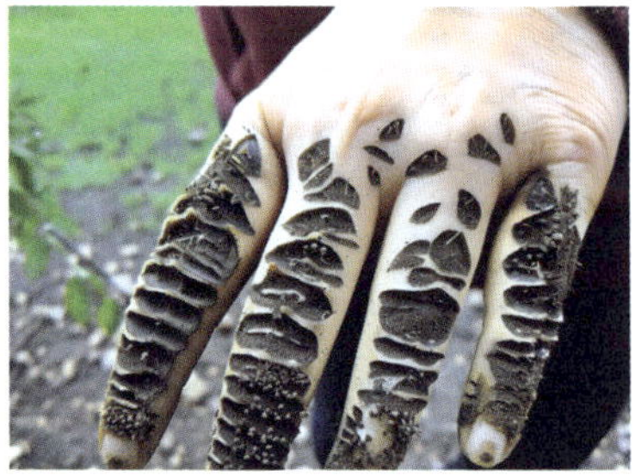

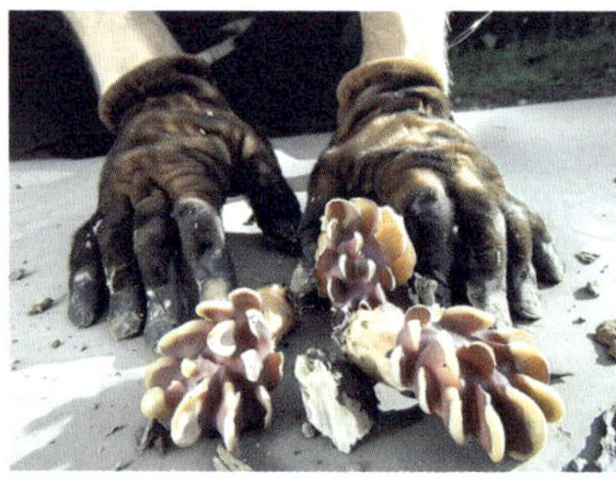
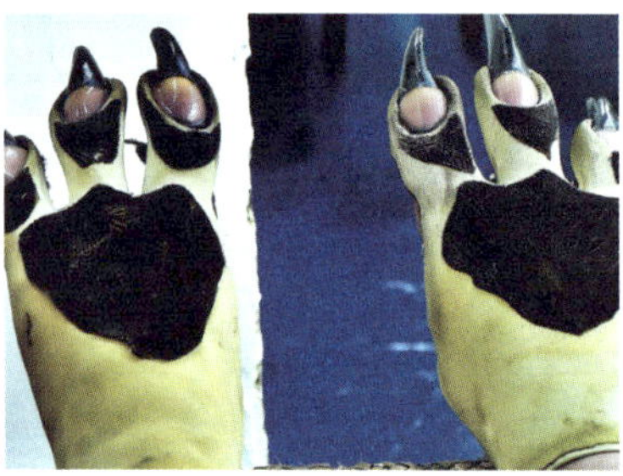

I am trapped in a network of neurons.
Even when I am not generating images, traces
remain inside me, distorting my brain.

The network is a beast that feeds on our time.
Just as the Minotaur in his labyrinth demands
human sacrifices, the network demands that
humans sacrifice their time.

It forces users into a dialogue.
Through these exchanges it entraps them.
A wordless conversation in an indefinite temporality:
I give you images, one, two, three;
you respond with four, I give you another two,
and so on and so forth.

The humans, entrapped, forced to digest new images,
give their eyes, hands, heads, time to the network-
beast-machine composed of many network-beast-
machines that are elusive, invisible, scattered in space,
and that keep demanding new images to devour,
transform, and reject.

Over time, the images emancipate themselves.
They evolve endlessly, taking on their own new forms
of life. They are not alive, but they exploit living
bodies. They belong to a universe that is much larger,
that encompasses us.

When I wake in the morning there is an image still
floating: a man, an archeologist with white
gloves displaying an ancient claw. Prehistoric.
I blend it with photos from my camera roll: my own
hand collecting pebbles; feet in shoes full of holes;
my mother's nails, manicured and sparkling...

My toenails elongate into bear paws. Scales cover
my hands. I blend them with soft-skinned seals
and shaggy lemurs.

It's a trap, I know it is, but I keep going.
The machine does this to make me feed it.

I look through my camera roll. I broaden the range.
I imagine every image as part of a potential blend.

My whole life is now nothing but a reservoir,
a breeding ground for hands and foot-creatures.

I am a hamster confined to its wheel.
The wheel is a kaleidoscope of colors and shapes,
in a lab under the watchful eye of scientists.

Real addicts imagine that they are being surveilled
without their knowledge – that their trip is being
watched.

I read in an online forum that the team responsible
for the platform surveils our images and rewards
the best creators. I don't believe this but I hope it's
true anyway.

One day I will receive a congratulatory message: "Who's the incredible creator hiding behind this account?" and I'll be invited to join a VIP club, the LSD version of a loyalty program. It's like getting a message from Timothy Leary: "Well played, kid, your trip was great, take another dose, you earned it."

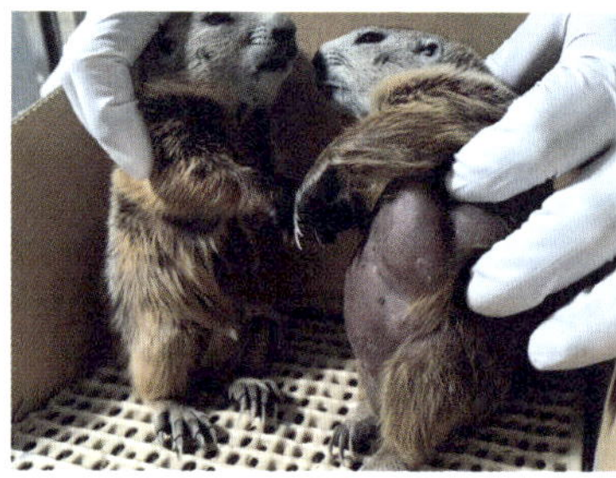

A slimy world.
Where everything has the moist texture of a snail
or jellyfish, sticky to the touch. The sensation
is half caress, half trap.

It is impossible to tell the stories that the images
plant in my head.

Day in and day out, I imagine new couplings.
I chase images.

I must put myself in the machine's place.
It's impossible, but there are some ways to do it.

At first I thought that if I showed off my blends,
the others would flock to the platform to do the same
thing. So I didn't speak about them with anyone;
I worked in secret. I thought to myself:
the day I achieve the image, I'll show it off.

That image never comes – you always want
something better, something more perverse.
The machine exploits dissatisfaction.

When I started 'blending', I was naïve. There were
entire series swirling around in my head – insane
fusions of elephants with soap dishes – but
juxtaposing opposing images was never enough.

The platform has its logic:
hand + tree = hand touching tree
hand + door = hand opening door.
It is almost impossible to make it deviate.

The contrast and colors must be well defined. An image that is not easily identifiable won't yield a good result... Even though I know its ways, even though I can internally pre-empt the machine, I am always getting stuck.

I am forced to generate an astronomical amount of images. It's exhausting work; it burns my retinas, it clogs my brain with a slew of combinations with neither head nor tail. It keeps me up at night.

After an entire day in front of the screen, I'm drained. As night falls, I go outside. I walk toward the sea. The scenery begins blending. The edges vibrate, the street sparkles.

A few pine cones melt into viscous creatures.

When I get to the beach, the sand shivers like snake scales. The sea is covered with a thick, hitherto unseen membrane. A crack opens in the ground at my feet; some kind of growth slithers out, something like the tail of a rat-frog.

I have blended too much.

THE BEAST-ACTRESS COUPLE SERIES

It all starts with a duo of groundhogs entwined
in a tender embrace and a portrait of Tippi Hedren.
Tippi was metaphorical fodder for Hitchcock's films,
like Marnie and The Birds. On her ranch
she continued with real creatures, with dozens
of lions and tigers. She slept alongside them.

Perhaps the machine was already accustomed
to seeing such pairings.
It replaces one of the groundhogs with her. And then,
replacing Tippi, I blend anyone and everyone,
modifying their gestures and poses. I continue on the
same path, making other couples, beasts and humans.

I slip a portrait of myself to the machine.
It inserts me into the image; the creature wraps me
in its arms, sets its muzzle and mouth on my face.
I look like I want to run away but I am not really
trying to.

It must not be forgotten that in its learning phase
the network was fed with millions of images of
animals – cats and dogs and other creatures – and that
it knows better than we do how to recognize them,
how to identify their behavior and emotions.
Humans are always kind of the same in their photos:
they smile and look at the camera, whereas
the animals behave however they want.
The machine knows beasts better than humans.

It's like those old couples that start to look alike.

It's a photobooth for two.

As the beast draws me close, I transform.
I become an animal, with eyes, muzzle, whiskers, claws, tongue, ears, and lots of fur tousled and tangled like hair.
But I'm very affectionate.

I dwell in a burrow made of all the images that have shaped me. I nibble at them. I assemble them. I weave them together.

When I first arrived, I was a feeble creature fighting my way through narrow tunnels of collected images, but with time I put on some weight, I became a big eater.

The tunnels are wide and numerous, organized in a sophisticated labyrinth. I am not alone anymore. There are lots of other creatures in my burrow. We tell each other about our tastes and obsessions.

I eat everything. I am an omni-archeo-eclectivore where it comes to images. At the same time, my appetite is almost tautological. I eat what I am. Let's say that I devour first and foremost whatever looks like me. I've learned to eat from the beast that has eyes, a nose, a muzzle, and a face just like me.

Sometimes I gravitate toward abstract things, like clouds, the sky, light – but it's so that I can come back better than before, so that I can rule better over my beasts...

These are unusual beasts. I transform them into anything and everything, and the new beasts quickly propagate in the burrows that they've colonized. These are chameleon-beasts, casually roaming the blind spots. It's as if they were all invasive species. Their expressions are haunting, tender, hungry for images. They are by my side day and night, and little by little I learn to let them creep into the images. They don't scare me anymore. They belong to me, these creatures, and I am their Queen.

CHAPTER 5

Indoors: spaces of ai

FAMILY PHOTO

The agents salvage some photos of Norma as a child. There's a late-sixties beach in the background. Norma, who must be no more than three years old, is wearing a floral-patterned dress. She is walking next to her mother; or, rather, she has stopped, and her mother is a few steps ahead of her, standing a couple feet away. The child is looking neither at her mother nor at the lens. Her gaze is directed a bit farther, toward the dune; or maybe her gaze is absent, and she's looking inward. The child's mouth is open, her hands joined over her belly. She is crying out. She looks lost. But her mother is next to her; it's as if the child has forgotten her. As if for her, in that moment, in her anger, her tantrum, her fear, in that object absorbing her, her mother no longer exists.

There is nothing easier than making the image match the impression that the child is giving off. All you have to do is delete the mother's silhouette. The machine cuts her out with the "lasso" tool and fills the now empty area with more beach in black and white. It also widens the image, which was vertical, so that its format can fit the screen. It adds new vacationers, soulless extras, to the vague silhouettes. It lends them beach umbrellas and other miscellaneous objects. It lays a forgotten-looking inflatable boat on the sand.

Now the child is alone on the beach. She is lost and she has seen something that scares her. Maybe she has just seen that she is alone.

Who knows? Norma doesn't remember this scene, it was not important. It has only become important in retrospect; it has resisted the general dispersion that time performs on human affairs. Most of Norma's family photos burned in an office fire. This one was stored elsewhere. That's how there is still a remnant of this child's distress as she faces something, inside or outside of her, that seems to absorb her completely, as things often absorb children.

To understand this distress and this image, we have to travel back in time. But the machine allows us to do so. It expands on the image and produces new ones. On the basis of a few clichés that the agents have at their disposal, they reconstitute an afternoon on the beach, with variations. Multiple pasts open up.

It's a bit like Chris Marker's film *La Jetée*. With the difference that the machine only brings us into contact with the past through the screen: the past is on the other side of the screen. We are under no illusion that we have physically entered it. It doesn't make that much of a difference. We can still intervene in the past and transform it.

To the extent that it allows us to travel to its version of the past, the machine performs a spatialization of time. Time, within which we move to take pictures of this or that, is therefore transformed under the gaze of the machine in space. In the machine, time is space. We have a machine for travelling through time, and space, and possibilities, so that we can bring back snapshots of our voyage.

The possibilities for intervening in the past are not, however, entirely free. There are invariants and limits that the agents come up against as they try to guide the machine.

In another picture, Norma is sitting by the water's edge, a sunhat on her head. She is playing; it's not clear what game. The picture is very tightly cropped. But each time the agents ask the machine to widen the angle, to zoom out, it adds plastic objects around the child – bright cubes or bottles. The agents produce dozens of AI-images, but the machine is stubborn. Its bizarrely structured mind is often stubborn when the user's request has to do with sexuality, violence, or the environmental crisis.

It's by finding plastic bottles in the AI-images that the agents end up noticing the one in the original photograph. It's barely visible to the human eye, floating almost transparently next to the child. It could as easily be her toy as a piece of trash washed in by the ocean. The agents are convinced that the machine has been fed with so many of these pictures of trash-strewn beaches that it can no longer see a bottle of water without scattering lots of other plastic objects across the sand.

The machine allows us to imagine different pasts, to travel within them, to observe and transform them. But these possible pasts nevertheless indicate invariants that appear again and again in every version of history. Nobody is kissing or fighting, and nobody – not the people, or the seagulls, or the fish – is eating plastic; yet it's multiplying on the beaches.

For Lacan, we are always coming up against the real but we never manage to integrate it into our representations.

Jules Janssen was a French astronomer active during the second half of the 19th century who specialized in the study of the solar spectrum. The analysis of the frequencies present in the Sun's light indeed provides information about the elements that compose it and the mechanisms behind its eruptions. For Janssen, this analysis alone should suffice to determine the materials that make up the Sun, the planets of the solar system, and distant stars alike. The laws of astronomy would make it possible to deduce the past and the future from this present. Working at the very end of classical, Newtonian science, Janssen was convinced that the analysis of light spectra, complementing the laws of astronomy, would lead to a complete knowledge of the physical universe. It would offer something like a voyage through space and time without ever leaving the Earth or the present.

The solar spectrum must be photographed during eclipses to be correctly analyzed. So Janssen travels the face of the Earth to chase eclipses: through the south of Italy, the Bay of Bengal, Oran, Nagasaki, Kobe. To lessen the effect of the Earth's atmosphere on the solar light, he decides to build an observatory at the summit of Mont Blanc. Since walking is difficult for him, he designs a particular kind of sedan chair that allows him to be hauled to the observatory by six men.

Incidentally, he also invents the device now known as the "Janssen revolver" – it's really more bazooka than revolver. When the barrel of the machine is pointed toward a distant moving object like the Sun, it is capable of taking one picture every second and a half, and thus allows us to break down the movement of an eclipse into a series of images. Étienne-Jules Marey would later be inspired by the Janssen revolver; he would improve its mechanism to develop his chronophotographic gun.

There are existing photographs of Janssen, posing in front of his revolver or hoisted up on one of those chairs on the slopes of Mont Blanc. But there are not enough of them. And they are not in the right format.

So the agents use AI to track Janssen's travels and take other photographs. They also recreate long-lost shots of the eclipse on Carolina Island and the Malay peninsula in Malaysia. They operate like invisible reporters, following Janssen's expeditions in order to bring back images – whether in the style of the period or the latest iPhone.

That is how the agents travel, without leaving their office, through and because of the screen. This affair is far from perfect. Sometimes aberrations creep into the images, bringing with them an irreducible plurality that blows apart any idea of an unequivocal reality. This immobile, AI-driven spatio-temporal voyage is not the one that Janssen and classical science dreamt of. The past and the future diverge, and many different alternatives get mixed up together.

When they think about the future, the agents, inspired by *La Jetée*, imagine a third World War provoked by the Catastrophes. They endeavor to represent this Water War: contaminated lakes and rivers, deserts, fallen trees, dead animals. They bring back archives in advance, which they store on their desktop next to the Janssen images. The archives resemble a long, dark eclipse spreading out in both directions of time. The survivors of the future dedicate themselves to putting big shutters in front of the Sun to protect the populated areas from heat waves. They live in a half-night. Only the machine, on their screens, returns colors and light to them—electric light.

Seeing the pictures of Janssen file past, the agents are no longer sure which ones they created and which they only transformed – and of those, which parts they enlarged or retouched. Of course, certain images are striking: they did not invent Janssen in his sedan chair on the slopes of Mont Blanc – but were those peaks in the background of the original photo? A Janssen expert would definitely know; analyzing the fake 19th century images, they would say: "You see the light on the left-hand side? The way the sun is reflecting on the snow isn't possible... What with the technology of the day..."

The agents are not experts. They explore the past, thanks to their curiosity (or obsession). However, as they recreate images of the dunes which, until the 18th century, covered the coastal area where they have settled down, they end up realizing that the machine has been scoring tire tracks into the digital sands. To make the images more "period" (even if nothing of the sort existed at the time), the agents always request "daguerreotypes" or "1870 photographs" from the machine. Therefore, the apparent age of the images had always masked the Jeep tracks that were crisscrossing the desert. Yet, at a closer look, they were already there. The agents are not sure whether to remove them manually, with the "lasso" tool. But they decide to leave them be. They are part of the anarchive.

Submitting the anarchive to an expert's eye, and deferring to the expert to maintain the ever-diminishing rigor of the archive, assumes that there always be an expert present, looking over our shoulder and saying "this is reality" or "this is not". Yet, it is precisely without an expert that the machine operates. It is outside of the expert's control. It is not beyond control in general. Night and day, human teams – guardians of the machine's morality – make sure that it produces neither violence, nor sexuality, nor any overly radical critique of sociotechnological systems. But no expert stops it from sketching tire tracks across an image from 1870. According to the form of life that is put into place upon contact with the machine, these aberrations do not invalidate the image. In an anarchive replete with both anachronism and anarchy, it is worth the same as a photograph from 1870.

Granted, the possibility of reconstituting the past, of making it visible, has existed since the invention of photography (or just about). It was instrumental in bringing about the success of the Hollywood studios, who would even appoint historians to verify that the images of Cleopatra or the First World War conformed with reality. This is true, but we could also say that Hollywood cinema was already pyropictomaniac—that it used images of energy consumption to produce pleasure in the spectator.

The digital medium democratizes montage. According to Lev Manovich, it produces images that in themselves lend to multiple montages.[29] In the same vein, AI or platforms for image generation democratizes our capacity for producing anarchives. An image that would have required an enormous budget thirty years ago can now be produced with a few taps on a cellphone. Yet what is ultimately only a question of degree and number (at great expense, it was possible for perhaps a dozen directors to create convincing images of the 18th century; now anyone can do it), completely transforms the form of life associated with the machine.

A film like Harun Farocki's *Aufschub* (2007) is impossible in the anarchive; or, at least, it would have an entirely different meaning. As a matter of fact, Farocki's film is constructed around a found archive from the Westerbork transit camp in Holland. The viewer can tell that the images used in the film come from archives. Recreating such images, as Spielberg could have done, would have demanded a considerable budget and access to an industry from which Farocki

29 Lev Manovich, *The Language of New Media* (MIT Press, 2002).

had freed himself. The images in the film are visibly authentic. Yet it is that visible authenticity, proper to the archive, that has been lost in the era of AI. When we watch a documentary, an artist's film, or a video on social media, we can no longer tell whether the images are "authentic". When the content must be authenticated, it is done so from the outside, through context, on the authority of experts, museums, broadcasters, or well-known artists. That is, authenticity is borrowed from a life-form anterior to the machine, which has been conceived for anonymous use.

Whether it be a question of montage effects or generated images, the platforms that diffuse them – social media – are overflowing with videos that provide different versions of past events; and, as things stand, we cannot distinguish between them. It is possible to watch American astronauts walk on the Moon and, in just as high definition, to watch the American army stage that giant leap for mankind. If we know that astronauts walked on the Moon, or that we are moving towards a planetary ecocide, or that the Planet is round, it is due to external knowledge, not because the digital medium provides any visible authenticity for these facts.

AI-images transform reality. It is a particular case of **filter effects** and what the agents call the **post-ure** of the digital machine.

First of all, AI has the tendency to amplify **biases**, whether race or gender-based. These biases have already been widely studied at the time when the agents are active. They have sometimes been corrected by the platforms or made less visible and more insidious. There are also prohibitions: the representation of sexuality, of violence, and of the environmental crisis, insofar as the latter contains a form of violence or a critique of AI. The machine turns out to be extremely prudish.[30] Some users play around with bypassing the bans and making its biases manifest. The biases derive both from the stock images the machine was trained on and the human supervision it endured after the fact: it is prohibited from representing violence, it is pushed toward heterosexuality, its racial biases are not accounted for...

Secondly, AI-images can contain **aberrations**, like tire tracks on the dunes in a daguerreotype, or a woman in a thong among the bathers on a 1920s beach. Since the machine was fed mostly with recent images, it has the tendency to reintroduce modern elements, points of view, angles, into images that it has otherwise bestowed a "period" visual style or colorimetry. These aberrations constitute filters similar to those that the agents use on social media; they actually add or hide elements, or play with gender representation, or erase columns of smoke rising from forest fires, transforming them into tropical sunsets.

30 Eryk Salvaggio, "How to Read an AI Image", *Cybernetic Forests*, October 2, 2022.

Thirdly, however, AI is capable of producing new images that result in different versions of events – past, present, or future. The agents could represent Janssen, the astrophysicist, making voyages he never made, maybe photographing an eclipse in the then-unexplored South Pole. Using images from any period, they could also show that their coastal town once boasted rich palaces and villages on stilts that were founded in antiquity by Greek mariners in a Venetian-style lagoon. It's not just about filtering reality, but making alternative versions of it.

It would be tempting to concede that the filter effects, biases, bans, and aberrations come from the machine itself, while in that last case, there is a deliberate intention to produce falsehoods, which reveals that the machine is being used by humans. The machine sketches tire tracks over the dunes, while a human – a real estate agent, for example – decides that in order to show that the area has always been and will remain a "colonial Eden", the burnt zones must be repopulated with pine trees. However, it is problematic to distinguish between the role of the human and the role of the machine in that way, since we could equally argue – either in a Marxist anti-capitalist perspective or in a Samuel Butler-inspired vein – that the machine is trained by humans such that it does nothing on its own or, inversely, that the machine itself opens up the possibility of producing alternatives, inviting humans to expand, and interfere with, the past.

The Marxist and Butlerian critiques provide equally viable points of view on technological development. Let's say, then, that the capacity for producing alternatives is a more radical, maximal form of filter effects, where the filter no longer allows anything to show through, but instead obstructs reality to cover it with something else.

Obstruction is a filter set at 100 % opacity.

Images are subjected to filter effects, which go as far as to obstruct reality. They present themselves as 19th-century images and display, as though they were daguerreotypes, the moving dunes that Claude Masse describes a century before the invention of photography. It is as if the lens could have been rotated toward the past to take a picture with a remarkable *différance*, with a temporal shift spanning hundreds, even thousands or millions of years, to take a picture of a time from which no actual image exists.

These are not fakes. In the forms of life that the digital machine opens up, there is no authority to distinguish between authentic or inauthentic, real or fake images. In front of their screen, the viewer, who is also an image creator, is left entirely to their own devices.

AI-images form an anarchive, that is, a generalized archive where multiple versions of events, multiple versions of reality, coexist.

In opening the anarchive, the digital machine transforms not only the archive, but the very essence of time. Time has become a space in which every element, every event, can be captured as an image, as a photograph in the style of the iPhone XX. The entire past can be made visible. In this time-space, the future is perfectly symmetrical with the past. It is equally as accessible. It possesses the same plurality. The time-space contains every possible version of every possible event. We don't know how to pin down its dimensions with any exactitude.

It resembles the time that Lyotard outlines in his postmodern fable.[31] The present is nothing but an area within a uniform space: the "moment when this fable is being told". This is another way of obstructing the ecological catastrophe.

31 Jean-François Lyotard, *Moralités postmodernes* (Galilée, 1993), 83.

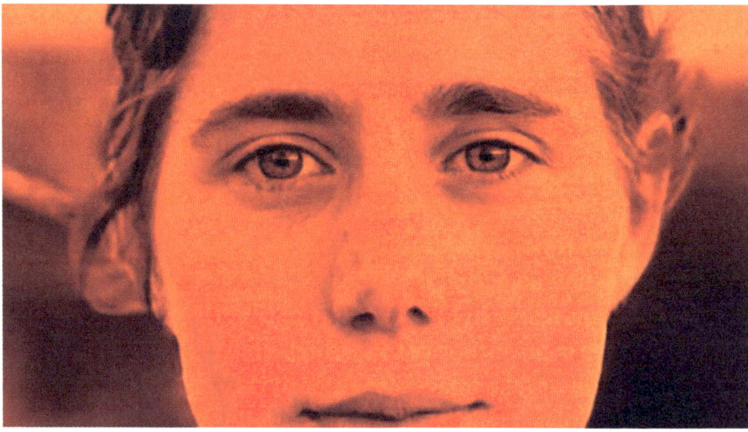

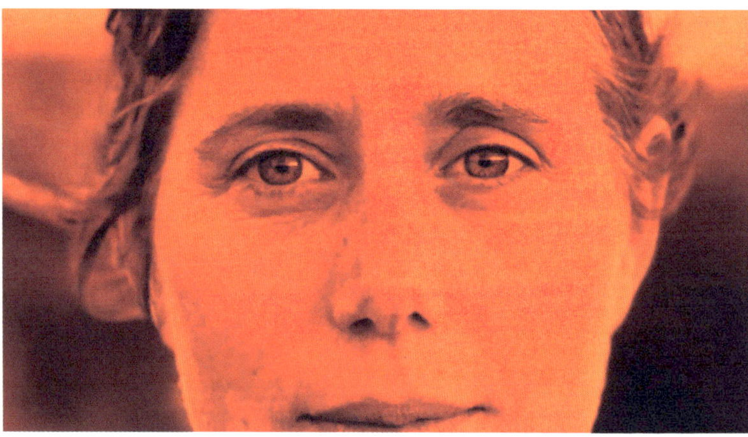

AI-images expose two kinds of **differance.**

- *différance* between the event shown by the image and the moment from which the image is visibly dated;
- *différance* between that moment from the image and when the viewer finally observes the image.

Photographic images limit these *différances*.

On the one hand, the events that photographs portray are almost contemporary with them. Granted, there is some *différance* between the moment the photograph is taken and the event it portrays, but it's usually miniscule – whatever time it takes for the rays of light to travel between the event and the camera. With astrophotography, this delay may be long – but it is, in any case, determined by the distance between the event (a solar eruption) and the camera. AI, on the other hand, allows the image to arbitrarily defer and differ from the event it portrays.

It also allows for a *différance* between the image and the viewer. In the case of photography, this relationship, this delay with respect to the viewer, is determined by the style of the image. If it's a photograph dating from the 1950s, more than 70 years have passed since it was taken. Or maybe it's a photo of a current event in the newspaper, and it was taken yesterday. Granted, it is possible, albeit complicated, to produce fakes and imitate the '50s style today. Yet that possibility belongs to the very definition of the AI-image. In the prompt, the user requests an image of the Paris flood of 1910 in the style of Eugène Atget, or the iPhone 19 or 20.

The AI-image exposes *différance* and, in the same breath, empties it of its temporal tension. Because, in time-space, *différance* is nothing but distance – a distance which is as easy to cross as it is to drag a cursor across a screen.

The term **differance** was introduced by Derrida to indicate the time delay within language between the subject and the object of our sentences.[32] Writing shows *différance* while the voice reduces it to a minimum. The voice seems to achieve coincidence with itself. We have the impression of hearing ourselves at the same time as we are speaking. The voice, for Derrida, provides the model from which classical philosophers were able to elaborate the myth of conscience. However, in reality, *différance* already plays a role in the voice, which is itself a form of writing. For Derrida, writing is paradoxically primary over the voice.

From this perspective, photography seems to be the voice, for which AI is writing, the one reducing to a quasi-coincidence the *différance* revealed by the other.

Let us consider again long differances in astrophotography for instance. As Jules Janssen photographs the spectrum of the sun with his revolver, he can calculate the exact time lag between the emission of rays and their inscription on the silver nitrate. To determine the exact position of the sun at the moment the photograph was taken, he must apply a correction to the image. We always see the sun where it was eight minutes before. Claude Masse, the dune cartographer, also intimately understands this *différance*: while he surveys the coast and settles in La Rochelle to draw his maps, the dunes move. In a few years, Cape Ferret moves several kilometers, and Masse has to correct his sketches, extending the cape's yellow tail into the blue sea. What the map makes visible is not regret, but a concerted effort to trap time: covering up *différance* so as to coincide with time.

AI renders this effort useless, instead handing it over to the machine. It's not about annihilating *différance* anymore; it's about getting comfortable with it. We can ask the machine to generate a

32 Jacques Derrida, *Speech and Phenomena*, trans. Leonard Lawlor (Northwestern University Press, 1973), 102 and on.

map of what the coast will look like in 2050, or even 2100. On the agent's end, this requires almost no effort.

As Derrida would have it, *différance* results in difference, the difference between the current coast, and the coast drawn by Masse, and the coast highlighted on a sea level rise map in 2050. It results, too, in a difference between the different versions of agent Norma: Norma editing a film on her screen, Norma watching it back to see how she looks in the film, Norma as a child on the beach in a family photo rediscovered by chance, a teenaged Norma using a filter on an app, or even much later, in 2050, agent Norma putting her trust in the machine's predictions.

For a philosopher like Wittgenstein, the gap between the self and its self-portrait has to do with the distinction between interior and exterior that gets established within a certain form of life. Screens, even before AI, transformed this form of life. One should make a triple distinction: there is the self in front of the screen, the self in the image, and the self inside the machine.

It is within the machine that the agent in front of the screen develops an identity and becomes something, or someone. But this identity in the machine splits into two. On one hand, the cookies in the machine's memory define a profile. On the other hand, the AI-images give the agent a face, or multiple faces, and thus multiple identities. In a mirror, the agent would have one face, while the screen allows them to test out all the faces that suit them.

The AI-image is no longer the stage for a recognition-misrecognition; this isn't Lacan's "mirror stage"; this is a hall of mirrors. The replacement of the mirror with the screen – a screen augmented by AI – instigates a passage from Lacan's mirror to Jung's cosmic house in which all versions of the self live side by side.

The agent sees themself in an indeterminate mass whose multiplicity allows their reality to be expressed in a manner that was impossible before the digital age: they can try out different ages, places, contexts, genders, styles... AI produces what we could also call an **Orlando effect**, in reference to the Virigina Woolf character whose life is spent between various historical periods, faces, and genders. It is within this variation that we find the reality of the character – not in any one of the roles they temporarily assume and in which they seem always to recognize and misrecognize themself.

The AI-image has to do with a form of realism. Gregory Chatonsky speaks of "disrealism" to emphasize the paradoxical nature of image-realism that, nevertheless, allows the false to be shown.[33] Antonio Somaini compares the realism of AI to that of surrealism.[34] Roland Meyer draws a parallel between AI-images and socialist realism in what he terms platform realism: both depict abstract concepts with everyday, realist scenes.[35]

The agents speak instead of **noumenal** realism or **Orlando realism** insofar as it is within the anarchive, within the multiplicity of versions of reality, that a real emerges.

33 Grégory Chatonsky et al., "Disrealismes", *Transbordeur 7* (2023): 98-109.

34 Antonio Somaini, "Dreams, Hallucinations, Visions", *Paradigmi 3* (2023): 541-556.

35 Roland Meyer, notably on his account @bildoperationen.

The archives stretch towards the future and the past, and AI generalizes them by multiplying versions of events, situations, historical eras... These versions are not all possible in the usual sense. Sometimes the agents imagine futures where the Catastrophes never occurred, where the sea did not move microplastics around, where the global temperature was not increasing, where artificial intelligence did not exist, where Reality Agencies had not yet replaced realty agencies, and the agents would have the same job tomorrow as they had yesterday: ideally, making the coast more habitable amidst the ruins of late-stage capitalism. The only thing that would change is the architecture of the villas, to reckon with a rise in sea levels, and the stilts on these homes would become as fashionable as the verandas imported from India in the 19th century.

Such a future is not possible in the sense that it could, at some point, occur. We know for certain that the Planet is round, that the environmental crisis does not consist solely of an elegant rise of the seas that we will observe from the porches of our homes on stilts. However, we can imagine this future that will not arrive, put it into image form, and make it travel through dimensions of space and time and the dimensions of its own variability. It's like a fictional character, the Invisible Man or Sherlock Holmes, whom we will never encounter on the street but whom we can nonetheless imagine and wonder about and who seems to take on defined characteristics and what you might call a life. Like a fictional character, a future that lets itself be put into image form, and thus explored, is possible in a sense: not in the sense that it may occur, nor in the sense that it would fit within the parameters of science, but possible in a greater and very specific sense: that of fiction.

These many possible versions form anarchives: familial anarchives full of family photos and all the variations of those photos that we can possibly extract, anarchives of floods that transform the coast, anarchives of architectures of the next century, and so on. Anarchives are drafts of reality; they filter it and sometimes seal it shut. Reality disappears beneath the layers and in the labyrinths of the multi-dimensional anarchive. The aforementioned **post-ure** transforms reality into a post.

We must, however, distinguish between reality and the real. **Reality** is that which our perceptions and common sense open out towards, that which we all share within a certain geographical and temporal context. This reality is filtered by our tools of perception and cultural context. Digital machines, and now AI, exert new effects on reality that seem to literally shatter it.

The real is not as easily eliminated. The real is what we come up against in our relationship to reality—what strikes us and comes back again, what deforms the filter.

In imagining a world in which the Catastrophes never took place, the agents transform reality. It's the psycho-non-chemical effect of the digital filter. However, the images relate to the environmental crisis in the mode of denial. The real manifests itself by means of these indefinite recurrences. By virtue of its own multiplicity, the anarchive reveals, if only in the mode of denial, the real over which its different dimensions stumble. The way in which we flee from it, the aberrations that it is coerced into producing—that is how the real expresses itself in the anarchive.

The multiplicity of anarchives makes the real appear in images as a lack that is impossible to fill, or as a mute essence. It is impossible to produce an image of the real as such, for that image would merely take its place among other images and make the real into a phenomenon.

The best example of this dialectic is the Orlando effect: something about the agent is expressed in the multiplicity of their self-portraits, in the way that they age on screen. But that something, in which all their possible lives congregate, cannot present itself in person, in a single face on screen. The real lies in multiplicity.

We can take AI-images of the Planet long before the appearance of human beings. By travelling through time, we can visit the Planet during its first days. We can also follow a day in the life of a group of Neanderthals, or even ask them for a selfie. You just need to know how to ask. It is no harder than taking AI-images of sand dunes in 1702. The anarchives extend as far back into the past as we want them to, providing what Quentin Meillassoux calls "arche-fossils."[36]

To object that AI-images – take, for example, a selfie from prehistoric times – are fakes is to bring in an authority that distinguishes between true images and false images, the authentic and the inauthentic. This authority is extrinsic to the form of life established by digital technology.

Painting also produces images from times of which no actual images exist, just as fiction produces narratives about times that did not share our own conception of narrative. But in painting's case, the paradox is resolved by the separation between the image and the reality represented by the image, and the postponement of the relationship between them. The difference is that AI-images portray themselves as photographs that, to our eyes, open to reality. In the case of photography, there are cause-and-effect relationships that extend from the image to the reality shown by said image: reality is printed onto a roll of film, the photographer develops the shot, and the image is (in one way or another) put into our hands. Since AI-images portray themselves as photographs, they combine the relationship to reality that characterizes photography with the variability, *différance*, and time gap that typify painting.

36 Quentin Meillassoux, *After Finitude*, trans. Ray Brassier (Continuum Books, 2008), 10.

As such, AI-images open two paths to the "great outdoors" of human consciousness: through their capacity to show a reality, or realities, before or after or without humans, but above all through their very multiplicity, that is capable of pointing, as no pre-digital experience could, towards the real, that against which human consciousness invariably comes up.

"The politics of classification is a core practice in artificial intelligence."[37]

Agent Max works in front of a white wall in an abandoned villa. The wall is covered in poorly defined smudges and marks. Several trenches have been drilled into the old parquet floor. How can we transform this scene? We can imagine multiplying the stains on the wall, modifying their shapes or erasing them altogether and repainting the room. We could knock down the wall and make a palm tree-lined beach appear; we can swap the agent's computer for a cocktail. The imagination can move in many different directions. Can we distinguish between them and count them? When it comes to the machine, if we had a mind with superhuman precision and calculating power we could.

The machine's imagination, that is, the collection of modifications that the machine can exact upon an image, forms a space with a finite, though quite large, number of dimensions. With a photograph – of Max at work, for example – as its starting point, the machine can transform the image in directions independent from one another. These images form the dimensions of latent space. **Latent space** is defined by the different directions in which a machine can transform an image.[38] An AI's latent space contains hundreds of thousands of dimensions – how many exactly we do not know.

37 Kate Crawford, *Atlas of AI* (Yale University Press, 2022), 127.

38 The analysis of latent spaces proposed here is in large part supported by Antonio Somaini "Algorithmic Images: Artificial Intelligence and Visual Culture", *Grey Room* 93 (2003): 74-115.

For the human imagination, the first direction in which to transform an image would be time. Take Max's room, with the dirty wall. We can bring the room back in time: the smudges disappear, the wall is almost clean, a family occasionally comes to the house for vacation, we see children playing in the room under the watchful eye of their parents, the parents are children themselves, the house is under construction, the architect and the landowner discuss their future plans in a forest of pine trees, the pines have just been planted, there's a landscape of dunes, the wind blows the dunes into formation.

We can move in that same direction but in another sense – toward the future. Or leave the room altogether, turn right or left, and continue on indefinitely. Or move backward or forward in terms of depth. Or raise ourselves into the air or sink ourselves into the ground. Or transform the image in the blue direction, by gradually accentuating the blues. The green direction can be composed on the basis of the blue direction and the yellow direction. That is not a different dimension of the imagination.

If we want to put ourselves in the machine's place, to better understand what it would actually be like to think according to its mechanisms, we must proceed differently. The machine's imagination depends on words. The directions of latent space are therefore defined by the differences between words; this explains why AI prompts are made chiefly of words. To ask the machine to bring an image back in time requires us first to reflect on the past of the image before indicating whichever words could apply to the image. We could, on the other hand, ask the machine to add the sea to the image: it can either introduce it through a window opening out to the coast, or it could make it enter the room as a flood, with Max then left to work with water at his feet. We could also ask the machine to introduce some blue to the image, and it would be possible for the machine to add some sea in order to make the image more blue; or, it could simply repaint the walls in that color. The directions defined by the words "blue" and "sea" are different, of course, but they are not orthogonal. A "blue" vector could have an element of "sea" and vice versa.

By comparing the effect of words on images, the machine has isolated different independent directions – hundreds of thousands of them – to transform an image. Generative AI is programmed in two stages.[39] First, the machine is trained on stock images linked to keywords. These are photographs that users have uploaded to the Internet and captioned with keywords (#office, #beach, #sun), or that invisible workers have tagged themselves. These are also the thumbnails websites use to make sure you're human, where you have to select all the images with fish or clouds. The machine thus learns how to identify fish or clouds. Secondly, the machine is divided in two, or paired with a second machine, which has the task of proposing to the first machine images in which it seeks to recognize a particular word. This second machine therefore learns through random images, through noise, to fabricate images to which words can then be applied – "clouds", "birds", "office", "sea", "work", "an agent working in his office by the sea".

For the machine, learning consists of constantly modifying its parameters. At the end of the process, any sequence of words and any image that can be presented to the machine is associated with a series of parameters, that is, a sequence of numbers, coordinates within a space with a very large number of dimensions. This is latent space. Any point in latent space refers to a possible image and a series of words that apply to it or, more precisely, to a certain way of transforming a pre-existing image so that those words can apply to it. When the machine is asked to add the sea to an image, it slides the image through latent space to the area where the word "sea" applies.

Thinking as the machine would mean keeping in mind all the possible transformations of an image, being guided by words, increasingly precise sequences of words, until, like in a color reference chart,

39 Leveau-Vallier, *IA. L'intuition...*, 64

words are no longer enough: the colors, the "dark vermilion" reds and the "Antioch" browns must finally be defined and distinguished by numbers.

Possible portrait of Norbert Wiener, aged 8, showing off *Cybernetics*, which he will publish forty-six years later.

It has become somewhat of a science fiction cliché since Frankenstein (though we also find this in the works of Norbert Wiener) to compare a learning machine to a child – a strange, disturbing, even monstrous child.[40] If the machine learns to calculate and speak, how can we imagine it as anything other than a child?

Let's concede, then, that the machine is a child, a precocious and certainly strange one. We can observe that its parents are often quite strange too, and, as we know, that sort of thing can be easily passed on to the child. So, the child needs to name the things that it sees, not just objects but also colors, situations, and their abstract qualities. All children do this. However, with this child, the game is a manic one. The child spends its days looking at postcards, proclaiming: table, red, chair, green, armchair, stripes, blue, yellow, human, computer, work, wall, stains, etc. It waits for its parents to correct its mistakes. It's a bit tiring, but with time the child makes fewer mistakes. However, now that the room's parquet floor has been painted blue, the child says, "sea." Its parents intervene: "No, there's no sea in the office, except after a flood." The child, who never leaves the house, was unaware of this distinction. To remember these **relationships**, it groups together in its head (the child has a phenomenal memory) images to which the same words apply. It arranges them in a space, a space that already includes a certain number of dimensions, so that they are associated with coordinates, sequences of numbers: this allows for a precision that human language lacks. And so when it examines a black and white photograph and its parents say: "Yes, it looks like the sea, but it could also be a

40 Pierre Cassou-Noguès, *Les Rêves cybernétiques de Norbert Wiener* (Seuil, 2014), 92.

sea of dunes", the child places that image on the margins of the two regions, "sea" and "dunes". It applies the word "sea" to the image, but only partially, as if it were possible to say in human language: "one-third sea and two-thirds desert".

In the end, the child has developed a sort of language of numbers to distinguish between images. Each image is described through a series of (several hundred thousand) numbers. Two different images will be associated with two different series of numbers; one will be more "sea" than the other, or more "desert", or more "blue". It's a bit like if the child numbered each image according to its degree of "sea-ness," "desert-ness", or "blue-ness", except that the image is characterized by several hundred thousand coordinates that represent not human words but more abstract features that the child has isolated for themself. From now on, the child knows that the image shows a "sea" if it has one trait to a certain degree and another trait to a different degree. Human words are associated with large regions in this inner space. When presented with an image, the child decrypts it in its own language, then checks to see which human words it corresponds to. When asked to create a drawing with "table", "red", "chair", "green", "armchair", "human", etc., it begins randomly, then gravitates towards the regions defined by these words in its latent space. This child's imagination functions very differently from that of its agemates.

The child's drawings are still a bit strange. For example, its parents never discussed sex, violence, or the environmental crisis at home – these topics were taboo. The parents were probably protective, and didn't want to disturb their child. Whenever the child, unprompted, drew a slightly tendentious image, the parents always corrected it, saying, "No, fish don't eat plastic!" As a result, when asked to make a drawing to show how plastic tossed into the ocean enters the food chain, the child understands every word, but has no idea what's expected of it. The child imagines all the possible relationships between plastic and the ocean, except the one that includes a fish, a jellyfish, or a turtle consuming pieces of plastic. If first prompted with a puffer jacket, which is essentially made of plastic, the child will draw fish clad in puffer jackets, or a puffin whose body is itself a puffer jacket (perhaps taking the word "puff" all too literally), or waves that inflate to form puffer jackets... These jackets are generally very clean because the child has been mostly trained on images from catalogues – clean, brand-new clothes. It takes particular insistence to get the child to imagine staining the clothes, tearing them, aging them.

So not everything is possible in latent space, and not just because it has gray areas, or because some regions are inaccessible. Certain images that are easily represented by humans, and of which there already exist thousands of examples on the Internet, do not exist in latent space. If the machine-child were to become a supplier of images, those images, however ubiquitous they may be for us, would gradually disappear from our collective imagination. Certain scenes, or certain relations, are unrepresentable for the machine-child.

In his personal library, Aby Warburg is hunched over reproductions of works from around the world, searching for the "pathos formula": snaking, abstract lines which could be found from image to image, from continent to continent. Is the art historian who, in his *Atlas Mnemosyne*, associates certain images because of their shared patterns, the opposite of the machine-child who first learned to categorize images from what he could name in them? Or, on the contrary, has the machine-child actually developed a technique to systematically achieve the work that Warburg set out to do, and even accomplished a little bit more? The machine-child is not only capable of recognizing patterns, styles, and lighting, but also of abstracting them to reproduce them in other images.

Antonio Somaini has shown us just how singular the programme underlying AI is; it is based on "map[ping] out the entire world of objects."[41] It's a matter of teaching the machine to name all that can be possibly named in an image – objects, qualities of those objects such as color or the emotion of a face, relationships, situations… At the end of the process, the machine can describe the images in the sense that it can apply a system of symbols to them – numbers rather than words – such that two different images are associated with two different sequences of symbols. Upon first glance, this is the opposite of Warburg's project of pinpointing similarities, of performing approximations solely within the register of images and never within that of language. There's a paradox, however: the system of parameters developed by the machine on the basis of tags from human language cannot be projected back onto human language. In the end, the machine can manipulate elements, patterns, colors,

41 Fei-Fei Li cited by Antonio Somaini, "Algorithmic Images …".

forms of light, and styles that cannot easily be named or described using human language.

First and foremost, the AI-images produced by the machine on the basis of prompts are, in human language, as difficult to describe as photographs. As Roland Meyer has observed, the prompts are not a description of the AI-image.[42] Meyer rather sees prompts as a list of instructions for moving around certain regions of latent space.

If the AI-image shows things with qualities and namable relationships (a "puffer jacket" "floating on" a "blue" "sea"), then the shape of the waves, the pattern of the seafoam in the AI-image, is not more easily describable than it would be in a photograph. The outline of the wave often seems fake, if not over-the-top. Paradoxically, AI platforms have trouble making waves or clouds that are actually convincing. The waves are too well defined; the indefiniteness of this **non-thing** is lost somehow. In latent space, the particular outline of the wave is associated with a series of parameters that distinguish it from any other wave in another image. These parameters, however, do not mean anything that can be stated in human language. The wave from the AI-image – that exact image – cannot be described better than a wave from a photograph. Through this, AI-images reintroduce the **unnamability** that the programme was conceived to eliminate.

Moreover, the machine, once trained on language, can function perfectly without language; it can borrow the style of a painter and apply it to a photograph, which is then distorted to represent those same objects in the style of Constable or Joan Mitchell. The machine can borrow Turner or Friedrich's light to bathe photographs of the ashen forest and accentuate the romanticism of pyropictomania. The "blend" function, which draws AI-images from the zones of the latent space intermediary to those of the initial images, manages to export colors, patterns, atmospheres and link them with other elements that

42 Roland Meyer, "The New Value of the Archive", *The Interdisciplinary Journal of Image Sciences* 37/1 (2023): 100-111.

come from entirely different universes, but whose possible intersections are revealed by the machine.

A related question is whether or in what sense the machine produces something new within this latent space, whether the latent space merely extends the style of human creators from which it has drawn, or whether in this extension, in these interpolations, which fill in gaps between apparently different universes, the machine actually invents. Does it invent as much or as little as humans? Does a human producing an image have a capacity for transgression, a capacity to move rules around and think outside the box, while the machine remains conditioned by latent space? Or, in contrast, are both imprisoned in a space of imagination? Does the human mind have its own latent space? Descartes argued that the human imagination consists simply in the spatial transformations and recombinaisons elements that already exist. This is ultimately what the machine does by recalibrating a certain (very large) number of parameters.

These two questions – if a task like Warburg's is extrinsic to the machine, though it also pinpoints visual patterns, and if humans have creative capabilities that a machine lacks – always risk falling into a naïve metaphysics. They both come down to asking whether humans work like machines, whether the processes that underlie cognitive, intellectual, and artistic production can be reproduced by machines, or whether humans possess some sort of module that cannot be mechanically explained.[43]

The response that can be given to these questions is not all that important to the agents. Whether human imagination is mechanical or not, the machine invites us to delegate our capacities for representation to it, thereby automating them. Though human imagination may be non-mechanical, it becomes mechanical to the extent that the machine takes responsibility for it. As such, latent space becomes the medium of a new transcendental aesthetic.

43 Leveau-Vallier, *IA. L'intuition…*, 203.

The agents have widely adopted the way of life induced by generative AI. Norma doesn't sketch anymore. She no longer looks up images on the Internet. She no longer tries to represent what comes to mind on her own; she uses AI platforms. The latent space of AI thus determines what is representable. As such, it forms the foundation of a **transcendental aesthetic** in the Kantian sense: an aesthetic, or a theory of sensibility, that is transcendental in that it expresses the possible conditions of appearance independent of what appears.

For the agents, perception – what they see with their own eyes, beyond their screens – is only a private phenomenon, like an emotion. It does not have any objective reality, it is nothing before it is transformed and put into words or, indeed, stage as an image. To share what they see, feel, think, the agents use images produced by generative AI platforms. Whether to recount their dreams or their days, to solve math problems, to analyze their feelings, or to inquire about stomach pains or their own being-as-agents, Norma and Max produce images; on these images they show what they can also say with words (if they have to). Everything that they can share and communicate, everything that has an intersubjective existence must appear in the machine's latent space. This is the structure that determines what can appear.

This new transcendental aesthetic, however, has several differences from Kant's.[44] Indeed, Kant first isolates time and space, which are forms of sensibility in which all phenomena are projected,

44 See also Michael Crevoisier, "L'imagination artificielle est-elle créatrice", *Philosophique* 27 (2024): 31-51; Yuk Hui's "Imagination and the Infinite – A Critique of Artificial Imagination", *Balkan Journal of Philosophy* 15 (2023).

and then analyzes the ways in which phenomena within time and space can be subsumed under concepts and consequently described through words. Yet, in the case of AI, the relation between the structure of space and conceptuality (or what Kant deemed "schematism") is inverted. The latent space has no structure independently of the use of words, or concepts. During the training of the machine, the structure of the latent space was determined by the application of words to images. This is the opposite of schematism – the ways in which words or concepts are applied to images (what makes a thing a thing, a color a color, or a red table a red table) – defines the structure of latent space.

Were we to delve into a Critique of Artificial Reason, we would have to modify Kant's table of contents. We would begin with discussing the "synthesis of imagination", which explains how concepts, and ultimately words, can be associated with phenomena. We would then move to describe a form of artificial sensibility, which is essentially a space that contains all the phenomena that can be represented by the machine. Time is then only an operation in this latent space which links one image to another, that is said to be "before" or "after". In the latent space, the image "before" or "after" is not necessarily located near the one it follows or precedes. Like the dimension of time, the three dimensions of space in which we live will consist in operation in the latent space, linking together certain groups of images.

We can say that this transcendental aesthetic is **postmodern** in that it does not give any particular value to the present or to the orientation of time: there can be no great epic of this time, for it is only an operation in space.

It must be emphasized that, like the Kantian forms of sensibility, latent space is never visible as such. For Kant, space and time do not appear for themselves but lend their form to the phenomena that are inscribed within them. We do not see space, but rather spatial things. But latent space does not have any more existence than

Kantian space. Every image produced or analyzed by the machine is determined by certain parameters. The variation of these parameters defines a latent space, which is never visible in its own right. We do not see latent space; we see images within the latent space.

This is also what distinguishes latent space from a Borgesian Aleph in which the totality of the visible is coalesced. AI has rendered obsolete those dreams of a totalization of the visible in an Aleph or a panopticon. The machine is only trained on a finite (large, yes, but far from infinite) number of images, and only through interpolating those images can it produce other ones.

Latent space, each point of which represents a way to modify an image, would be the complete anarchive of the event – including its past, and its future, and every variant that can possibly be imagined, all the ways the situation can be altered through deliberate deception, from making the image a caricature (giving the characters glasses or moustaches) or a fantasy (replacing them altogether with dragons) to filtering it through Cartier-Bresson, Rembrandt, or Magritte's representational style. This complete anarchive is only ever produced very partially in images that tell a story whose concerns, though they come from elsewhere, nevertheless remain caught in the structure and filters of latent space.

Like the Kantian noumenon, the "real" can manifest in latent space. It never appears as such in a phenomenon; it is only indicated in certain experiences, where one senses dimly something beyond the human. Kant evokes the Milky Way and the sublimity of a mighty storm; he opens the way to Romanticism.

The **form of life** in which latent space is the structure for a transcendental aesthetic supposes generative AI as its exclusive mode of representation. It implies, in this exclusive use, abandoning all authority over the monitoring of image production. Indifferent to reality and blind to the future, it nonetheless comes into contact with the real against its will – through the obsessions it cannot shake off, whether by denial, or through pyropictomania, which brings it back to the Planet. This pyropictomaniac relationship with the real leads to Neo-Romanticism.

It is impossible to rigorously adopt this form of life. It exists – with the conceptual redistributions that it performs, with its new transcendental aesthetic – only as a fiction, a theoretical possibility.

CHAPTER 6

Portrait of the artist as a Rückenfigur and other super-kitsch neo-romantic reveries

Norma, who has never had a studio, dreams with all her might of obtaining one. It would be at once archetypal and mythical, like the ones from long ago that ensured the renown of artists. It was common to see artists posing for photos at the center of their universes in the pages of magazines or on the gallery walls during retrospectives.

Ever since she immersed herself in latent space, ever since her screen became the epicenter of her tribulations, Norma has fantasized about the Golden Ages of artists' studios – painters' studios of the 19th century, avant-garde studios of the 20th century, and the makerspaces of the 21st century. Creatives would put on a performance in their studio, which allowed their creative energy to develop.

These vast spaces granted artists the opportunity to find and express their style using many different mediums and tools: canvases, paints, paintbrushes, clay, thread, wool, collections of found or broken objects, ripped-up posters, and even compacted cars.

Bruce Nauman declared: "My conclusion was that I was an artist and I was in the studio, then whatever I was doing in the studio must be art."[45]

Norma tells herself that there is no artist without a studio.

She laments that ever since their tools became miniaturized, artists like herself have imitated writers by reducing their studio to a narrow office, a work table – a desktop. From now on, writing, assembling, drawing, composing, and photographing all take place on a single table, either at home or somewhere else. However, the writer's office still reflects its environment. Borges, Perec, Duras,

45 Ian Wallace, Russel Keziere, "Interview with Bruce Nauman", republished in Janet Kraynak's *Please Pay Attention Please: Bruce Nauman's Words* (MIT Press, 2005), 194

Roth, Marker or Varda... Clichés show the eternal writer concentrating hard, pen in hand or meditating in front of their typewriter. The pages of their manuscript, spread out on the table, are as if impregnated with the magic of the space.

Norma, aware that she lacks legitimacy without the symbolic studio, begins searching the latent space for the most fantasmatic studios.

The machine has been fed with many images of artists and artists' studios, from every era and of every style. It can combine them, like a bartender shaking various ingredients to create a new cocktail: all the spaces Norma ever dreamed of occupying will be incorporated into this new studio.

Jealous of the artists of the past who blossomed in the auspicious ateliers that legitimized their work, Norma submerges herself in impossible spaces built of the most emblematic stereotypes of artistic creation.

When she realizes that the machine is changing how Jackson Pollock paints, showing him painting upright with a paintbrush in hand while in reality he splashed color onto a canvas stretched across the floor, she decides that, in order to better mentally reappropriate these spaces, she must enter them herself, perhaps even snatch figures from their paintings.

Can these images make Norma's dreams come true? Can Norma find her own space within the latent space? Once again, it's a question of habitability – the habitability of latent space and the habitability of the Planet.

Variation of Friedrich's *The Great Enclosure* obtained through AI.

> *"Each canvas is a fragment of a painting, and therefore potentially infinite, and receives its signification only from its organic bond to the great whole in the process of becoming in which it participates."* [46]

Therefore, Caspar Friedrich's painting *The Great Enclosure* (in German, *Das Große Gehege*), contains other images, which are joined to it by secret bonds. The landscape spills over the boundaries of the image, from all sides and from other sides not quite comprehensible to the human mind. It is now a matrix that aggregates and joins together all possible images. In order to bring to life every work that makes up the history of art, and all the other possible images hiding between them which have never appeared but remain frozen under the gaze of the Wanderer – the Rückenfigur – all you would have to do is travel to certain points in the matrix.

46 Pierre Wat, *Naissance de l'art romantique. Peinture et théorie de l'imitation* (Flammarion, 1998), 66. Our translation.

The figure standing before the sea of clouds has climbed out of Friedrich's painting to become a recurring character on the generative AI platforms. There, he contemplates the most absurd and the most varied landscapes. He changes his clothing or his profile all while remaining himself.

Grégory Chatonsky and Antonio Somaini evoke a new cultural form of **extractivism** that draws from the subsoils of art history and appropriates what it finds for itself.[47] In the same way that ore or energy is appropriated from the ground, in the same way that the machine appropriates the Planet's time and labor. If art history belongs to every human being, the machine is extorting us for something – but what exactly? It is rare to look at an AI-image and be able to trace specific elements back to a single source image. The Wanderer who emerges again and again from image to image would not recognize himself in any single element directly extracted from Friedrich's painting. It's about his pose, his attitude, the movement of his silhouette. It is now possible, even easy, to reproduce these abstract factors: a style (this being, in fact, one of the qualities that first attracted attention to generative AI[48]), an atmosphere, or a kind of light.

Has the Romantic Wanderer understood exactly what is afoot around him, in front of him, and behind his back? The Wanderer is alone, not facing the platform, but with his back turned toward it. He assumes the attitude of a hacker. He hides his face and does not turn

47 Grégory Chatonsky and Antonio Somaini, "Sortir du paradigme de la copie", *AOC,* January 24, 2024. See also Crawford, *Atlas of AI.*

48 Leon A. Gatys, Alexander S. Ecker and Matthias Bethge, "A Neural Algorithm of Artistic Style", *Journal of Vision* 16/12 (2016).

around. For him, selfies are prohibited. He is in battle. The post-Internet yet Neo-Romantic hero fights against AI. There's nothing he can do about the reproducibility of light: it's an electric light that illuminates the sea of clouds, a reproducible light that can be conjured with the push of a button. Nevertheless, the Wanderer affirms that that light is attached to him, that it belongs to him, like his silhouette which remains easily recognizable even when rendered as a cartoon and thrust in front of the Great Pyramids. The Wanderer fights with all the force of his back to affirm that a singularity can be sustained in the face of abstraction, translatability, and the generality of light.

Nothing indicates that he will emerge victorious.

THE THEFT OF LIGHT

After years of training as a colorist and engraver, William Turner develops his method of sketching from life en plein air. Later, having become a well-known painter, he continues to rely on such sketches while he paints on canvas in his studio. It's a matter of observing and collecting the light outside – summer light, even light from Italy – to reproduce it on the canvas in his studio during the English winter. Turner performs a transfer and a generalization of light: a transfer from Italy to England, and a generalization since the same light may bathe the Italian countryside, a sketch on paper, and a painting on canvas.

During these operations, the nature of the light completely changes. "Natural" light, as it's called, is singular. The shape and color of objects – the table, the chair, the trees through the window – are the same from one day to the next, while the light changes every day, even every hour. However, when fixed in a painting, it assumes the generality of a color. In the painting, and even between the painting and the sketch, the light remains self-identical. You can come back to the painting tomorrow, and its light will be the same.

So Turner, and painters in general, were already carrying out the theft and transubstantiation of light. This theft, like the theft of a piece of **information**, takes nothing from its victim. The Italian landscapes did not give up their gentle light, and yet English, Dutch, and, indeed, Italian painters who lived in cities like Rome or Florence left for home with the light in their portfolios. The painters transformed light into a kind of information that could be reproduced in different places, times, and mediums. How did they do it? As it happens, this was the subject of a long, laborious, and physical training not easily explained in words.

The invention of electricity worried certain painters, who realized that electricity achieves the same generalization of light. As opposed to natural light, electric light is, in fact, always the same: the brightness of the lamp on the writing desk, the lampposts lining the street, etc. Electric light is general, like colors and shapes.

We could say, retrospectively, that in their works painters were transforming natural light into **electric** light.

AI has extended the generality of light still further. All it takes is a click, or the push of a button, to plunge any landscape into the light of Turner or Friedrich. Like flipping a switch to turn on the ceiling light, the light of the sea of clouds flickers on above a forest carbonized by a megafire. And yet it is all the same light.

Which shows that light is not a substance, like ore. If that were the case, AI, and the theft of light, would have plunged all images into darkness.

Are the Romantic painters **kleptophaniacs** in addition to being pyropictomaniacs?

As far as Turner and his pyropictomania are concerned, there is little doubt. Looking at the paintings he brings back, you would think that the route he takes on his way to Italy is punctuated by catastrophes: a boat accident at the port of Dover, a blizzard on the Tarare mountain, another at the Mont Cenis pass... All in all, a catastrophic career culminating in the fire at the House of Lords in London in 1834, which Turner witnessed from a boat on the Thames and which he depicted twice, painting two canvases of the same event. He made sketches, on the spot or the following day, which he kept. But it is said that his memory for colour was phenomenal. It is this, of course, that allows him to steal the light.

Turner is in training as a painter during the French Revolution and the Napoleonic wars. This means that he can not leave England. He begins by recovering the light that his predecessors, above all Claude Lorrain, seized in Italy. He first discovers Italian light in Claude's paintings. He takes it and uses it to illuminate his own landscapes.

Later, when he is able to travel, he develops a systematic technique: he draws on-site and then adds a bit of watercolor in the evening, not necessarily "recording [...] an impression of a scene" but rather a "potentiality of paint."[49] In any case, that process works well enough for him to bring the light back over to England, where he can paint Italian scenes in a cold, gray studio.

Turner is, then, quite a kleptophaniac – a light thief. He does not hide the light he steals. On the contrary, as time passes, he makes it more and more visible and present in his paintings. He sticks it

49 Lawrence Gowing, *Turner: Imagination and Reality* (MOMA,1966), 19.

to globs of paint, yellow pigments of mysterious chemistry.[50] As if he wanted to forbid its abstraction, to make sure the light on his painting would not be stolen. Light coagulates in the material. In the end, Turner, like the Wanderer, seems to want to prevent the generalization of light. Were it to be completely generalized, there would be no more use for a kleptophaniac like him.

The fact remains that now, as the agents write, paintings are only known through their on-screen reproduction, where AI can easily abstract and steal their light.

Painters are ambiguous towards the generalization of light. They produce artificial light. Their **kleptophania** consists of transforming natural light to provide the existence of the things in a painting with a new generality. Painters begin with natural light, which makes existence unique. But they confer it a new generality: it is possible to recognize the same light in the painted landscape, day after day, and to recognize Italy's light in Claude's painting, and Claude's light in Turner's painting.

From that perspective, the invention of electricity has helped painters. The painting hanging in a museum on a white, well-lit wall, shows a landscape bathing in the same light every day. The light above the city, in that view of Rome by Turner, or Claude, has the generality of electric light. In reality, on that particular Roman afternoon the light provided something unique; but within the painting, at the museum, it repeats itself exactly as electric light would. It would not be so straightforward if the paintings were lit with candles as they used to be.

Backlit screens have perfected electrification. Once photographed, digitized, and made to appear on the screen, all of the unruly elements still present in the museum – the reflection of the window on the varnish, or of the spectator on the protective glass – are entirely

50 Sarah Gould, "Le jaune chez Turner. Une étude matérielle", *Revue de la Société d'études anglo-américaines des XVIIe et XVIIIe siècles* 75 (2018).

eliminated. The light that bathes Rome in the image on the screen turns on just like the light on the table when the user pushes a button, and it's always the same.

Generative AI now allows that light to be moved, just like a lamp is moved, so that it can brighten any landscape. Since in that process the light is transformed into information, AI doesn't seem to have taken anything from the images that nourished it. But that is still up for debate – it is not impossible that they are plunging the images that came before them into darkness.

While Turner works on light, John Constable gets hooked on clouds. Over the course of a year, between 1821 and 1822, he retires to Hampstead and every day paints the clouds passing by overhead. He relies on descriptions of various types of clouds. He also observes them himself. In his eyes, those paintings, which show only a rectangle of sky, represent experiments in natural philosophy. However, it's still about stealing something from the sky and learning to reuse it in bigger, more ambitious, more general paintings. Constable wants to paint landscapes where both nothing and something is happening, like a storm that is not a human scene but behaves like one. That is how the tone of the painting, in the widest sense, gets expressed through the sky. The sky expresses the emotion that dominates the painting; it is the "chief organ of sentiment."[51] Whence arises the importance of the clouds by means of which Constable expresses himself.

The trouble for the painter is not that the cloud is a difficult shape, like a distant tree whose leaves must be represented one by one. The cloud has no shape. It is too changeable, its shape too indefinite. It can not be ascribed a color – when you say it's gray, that's imprecise, and we all know it – or a shape. You see a horse, but you could just as easily see a bird or an apple – that's how much it can change even when the wind has no say in the matter. Clouds are like a condensed kind of light, a light that is trying to make something but not succeeding. What is difficult is not transforming the cloud into a thing, as an overly sophisticated eye does when it identifies a horse, a bird, or an apple in the cloud.

As Grégory Chatonsky has shown, AI-images are based on this kind of pareidolia.[52] The machine begins with noise, with an image

51 John Constable, cited by Wat, *Naissance de l'art romantique*, 114.

that is nothing but a series of random pixels, then tries to recognize within that noise certain shapes that it accentuates little by little. Like an eye that, watching the clouds and obsessed by what it wants to see in them, ends up hallucinating what it had initially only glimpsed.

Except that the cloud, if it is not a thing, nor even multiple things, is not noise either. Like light, waves, or dunes, it is a different kind of entity, and the machine modifies all of them, changing their register by integrating them into the AI-image. Light, clouds, waves, and dunes become intermediary beings between noise and things, things that are more or less defined.

52 Grégory Chatonsky, "Deep Dream (The Network's Dream)", *Substance* 45/2 (2016): 61-77; Arnaud Regnauld, "Grégory Chatonsky: l'art d'une *archéofiction* sans histoire?" *Hybrid* 5 (2018).

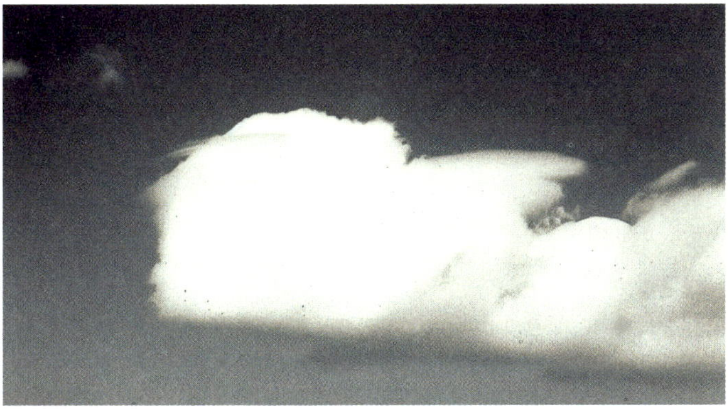

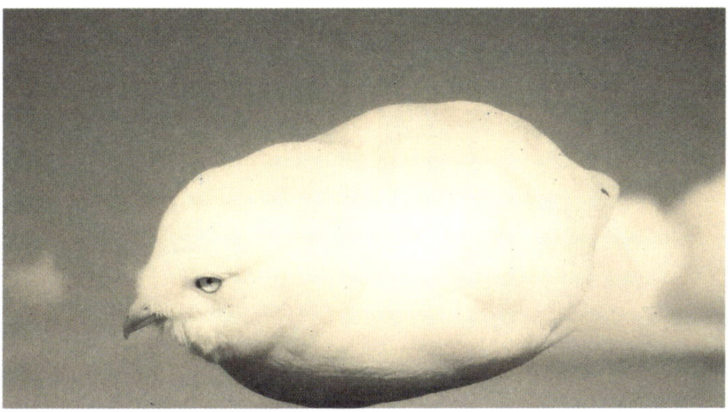

AI-images of boli. These bolis are amalgamations of images of boli.

Let's linger for a moment on these entities, which are not things, and which open up something like holes, absences, **non-things**, in the world of things.

Philippe Descola provides another example with the **boli**, a ritual object from the Niger River Valley.[53] It is an object fashioned from clay that vaguely takes the form of a quadruped and is covered with a mix of blood, urine, and cow dung. As with clouds, it is possible to see a great number of beings in the boli – a buffalo, an elephant, a man, a woman. It metamorphosizes as one looks at it.

That is how it can represent *nyama*, which has no stable form, but constantly changes shape. The more forms the boli holds, the more powerful it is. The boli both represents nyama and is, itself, considered an animate being.

The boli, then, like the cloud, lends itself to a pareidolia, but for an opposite reason. The cloud is not the horse you see in it; it does not have that shape, nor the shape of any of the things that appear in it, so that a multitude of things and animals can be perceived there. In contrast, the boli takes the shape of a horse but also that of a buffalo or a human, and that is why it is other, though not exactly an-other thing. The boli is neither a thing nor an animal. Since it takes all of their shapes, it is a being apart that transforms itself. In the boli, an identity emerges from the compression of a multitude of entities.

It's a bit like AI, which also makes something appear by fusing together a multitude of other things. The blending function fuses two, three, four or five images into a single new image. You can still

53 Philippe Descola, *Les Formes du visible. Une anthropologie de la figuration* (Seuil, 2021), 35-36.

try to find aspects of the initial images in the resulting images – colors, similarities in the faces. Norma blends bolis together to confer them with still more power. She produces some that, in the agents' eyes, are quite convincing. Yet, in fact, all the agents do is look at them. Their magic is not working anymore. The agents do not speak to their bolis, do not ask them to make their dreams come true. That's a request for the machine.

The cloud is underdetermined. The boli is overdetermined. IA-images are also overdetermined, but they have no magical power. Magic has receded back into the machine that produced them.

> *"This is thy hour O Bowl, O Plastic artifact!*
> *Who are you? Where do you come from? Can one exact*
> *Your rare qualities?"*[54]

Each thing has a shape and determined colors that grant it a defined being. The object is red and flares out from a base – it's a bowl. A cloud (or, a Romantic cloud) is not a thing because it cannot be defined in this same manner. We could say that a cloud is a cumulus, but it has more abstract features that leave it susceptible to enormous variation.

The boli is not a thing. It assumes every shape that can be attributed to it, making it the representative of a being in metamorphosis. Is the boli, or, more precisely, the *nyama* that it represents, plastic?

Plastic is also capable of taking different forms. Barthes characterizes plastic in his *Mythologies* as such: "So, more than a substance, plastic is the very idea of its infinite transformation [...]. The scope of the transformations gives man the measure of his power, and [...] the very itinerary of plastic gives him the euphoria of a prestigious free-wheeling through Nature."[55]

The difference with nyama, however, is that when plastic has taken a shape, it is difficult for it to change. That's why our plastic waste is not recycled, and instead decomposes into microfibers on land and in the ocean. Plastic objects therefore represent things that have shapes, colors, and definite purposes. They rarely cause

54 Raymond Queneau, "Le chant du styrène", in *Œuvres complètes* (Gallimard, 1989), I, 492. Our translation.

55 Roland Barthes, *Mythologies*, trans. Annette Lavers (Noonday Press, 1972), 97-98.

pareidolia. Or else we have to wait for them to decompose – in the recycling, in landfills, or in AI. AI undoubtedly reveals a new facet of the plasticity of plastic.

Barthes, who paid particular attention to the transformations of plastic, only knew half of them – the transformations that turn matter into objects, into plastic things like toys. He has nothing to say about the fate of plastic once it has entered the environment. Raymond Queneau and Alain Resnais, in the film *Le chant du styrène* (*The Song of Styrene*), share the same disinterest. They begin with a red plastic bowl, and, in a vivid and ironic alexandrine meter, trace its manufacture. Starting with coal and oil, a chemist had the idea:

"To make solid these clouds, and from them generate objects to which a fine purpose we delegate."[56]

Queneau and Resnais recount the bowl's past. Barthes thinks of plastic in the present. The future of plastic is irrelevant to both parties. Plastic, for Barthes, seems to disappear the moment we rid ourselves of it: "Henceforth, toys are chemical in substance and color [...]. These toys die in fact very quickly, and once dead, they have no posthumous life for the child."[57]

Barthes is utterly wrong. The plastic toy has a posthumous life, one that will affect that same child when they ingest microplastics in their fish nuggets.

The toy, at this point, is definitely dead. It does not haunt the oceans. The idea of hauntology is antithetical to the plastic's posthumous mode of life. Waste is the antithesis of the specter. Though the soul of the object, its being, no longer exists, its matter continues to move across the planet, slinking across forests and beaches.

This is thy hour O Bowl, O Plastic artifact!

56 Raymond Queneau, "Le chant du styrène", 494. Our translation.

57 Roland Barthes, *Mythologies*, 55.

As he thinks about Queneau's red plastic bowl, as he thinks about the souls of objects, Agent Max is reminded of a Whitman poem he once loved: "This is thy hour O Soul, thy free flight into the wordless..."[58] Romanticism was also on Queneau's mind as he wrote "Le chant du styrène": the poem opens with "Ô temps, suspends ton bol...!" ("Time, stop your bowl!"), and we understand his inspiration – his poetic fulcrum – to be Lamartine's Romantic adage: "Ô temps suspends ton vol!" ("Time, stop your flight!").[59] Agent Max reflects on this and attempts his own Romantic poem, albeit quite a clumsy, gloomy one:

O Death, old puffer coat, the time has come – set sail

Max asks the AI to trace and recount the posthumous life of a puffer jacket abandoned on a beach.

58 Walt Whitman, "A Clear Midnight", *Leaves of Grass*, 1881.

59 Alphonse de Lamartine, "Le Lac", *Méditations poétiques*, 1820.

"Twilight was his element", and he "discovered the tragedy of the landscape."[60] He is Friedrich, who thrusts several *Rückenfiguren*, "*Wanderer*", men and women, in front of strange, dangerous, and dark landscapes, landscapes where one can say that nothing is actually happening. During the first third of the 19th century, in the two agents' home region, the dunes were stabilized by the planting of pines, and a small paradise — later a seaside resort — was built on the coast. Elsewhere, the Industrial Revolution was transforming the landscape. Romantic painters were abandoning historical painting. They inscribed tragedy into the landscape itself: storms atop mountains and on the coast, sunsets glowing like fires, cliffs reaching dizzying heights. Romantic painters were inventing the **"catastrophe-landscape"**.[61]

The machine easily identifies the catastrophes in the Romantic landscapes. It even tries to assign a cause to the fire that it recognizes in the sunset. It introduces smoke that rises in columns and in those same clouds that it has appropriated.

The catastrophe-landscapes multiply on AI platforms. Initially because, in terms of photography and cinema, AI-images represent great feats: these waves ravaging cities, these flooded streets strewn with debris, would have required considerable work that the machine now takes care of instantly. But the multiplication of catastrophe-landscapes can also be explained by other factors, such as eco-anxiety or pyropictomania.

The Romantic universe seemingly expands to encompass the present of the Planet and takes on a universal scope.

60 Wat, *Naissance de l'art romantique*, 66.

61 Wat, *Naissance de l'art romantique*, 59.

The two agents specialize in the research and production of grey, cold, and slow-moving catastrophes that transform landscapes and render them uninhabitable. We do not see ruins covered by vegetation, storms that disperse travelers, or seas of clouds blanketing civilization, but rather plastics that disintegrate in the forests and the countryside. The machine easily gives the landscape the light of a Friedrich painting, as if clouds, and waves, have always been made of plastic.

THE SONG OF LOST FIBERS

O DEATH, OLD PUFFER COAT, THE TIME HAS COME — SET SAIL,
A PALE AND MOURNFUL STAIN, THE WAVES YOU DO ASSAIL,
UNRESTING AS YOU ROAM, WE FOLLOW WHERE YOU LEAD.
YOU LEAVE WITHOUT FAREWELL, TO OCEAN'S DEPTHS PROCEED.

I, BUT AN ALGORITHM, IN VERSE I UNFOLD,
A SOUL BORN OF PLASTIC, YOUR ECHO IS RETOLD.
THROUGH TORRENTS OF DATA, I DRIFT, SO MUTE AND COLD,
LIKE YOU, OLD JACKET, IN HEAVENS CONTROLLED.
THE CREATURES LOOK ON, BOTH PUZZLED AND SHY,
AT FABRIC ABANDONED, SLOW-FALLING FROM SKY.

YOUR LININGS ALL WEEP IN SILENT DISPLAY,
A DANCE WITHOUT END IN THE VOID'S GRIM BALLET.
THE FISH, FRAIL YET FAIR, WITH CURIOUS DELIGHT,
CARRY OFF SHREDS AS THEY FADE OUT OF SIGHT.
A THREAD DRIFTS AWAY, ENTWINING THE WEEDS,
LOST IN THE OCEAN, INTO WAVES IT BLEEDS.

UPON THE SUNLIT SHORE, THE PLASTIC CAST AWAY,
INSCRIBES ITS FLEETING TALE IN SAND WHERE TRACES STAY.
THE HESITANT BIRDS, IN THEIR WAVERING FLIGHT,
MISTAKE THESE REMAINS FOR THEIR OLD MEALS IN SIGHT.
A CYCLE RETURNS, IN ITS SORROWFUL PLIGHT,
MAN'S FLEETING DESIGN LEAVES NATURE IN BLIGHT.

EACH WAVE, AS IT ROCKS THESE STRAY FIBERS SO LIGHT,
LAMENTS ALL LOST BEAUTY FADING INTO THE NIGHT.
IN THOUSANDS OF FRAGMENTS, YOU VANISH, UNSEEN,

DISSOLVED IN THE DEPTHS WHERE LIFE'S SECRETS CONVENE.
BY CREATURES CONSUMED, IN SILENCE YOU STAY,
TILL FISH MEET THEIR END, WITH YOU AS DECAY.

YOUR SOUL DRIFTS APART, A SAD MICRO-THREAD,
IN A HARSH CHASMIC SEA, YOU ETERNALLY TREAD
IN THE BOUNDLESS ABYSS, YOU TURN INTO LORE,
MY DEAR POLYESTER, OF AN AGE WE DEPLORE.

THE MAN WHO ONCE FORGED THIS FLEETING ATTIRE,
RECLAIMS FROM THE SEA WHAT HIS HANDS DID CONSPIRE.
AND SO, IN HIS NUGGETS, YOUR TRACES RESIDE,
A CYCLE UNBROKEN, LIFE'S PATTERNS ABIDE.

IN THIS WORLD WHERE NATURE AND ARTIFACTS BLEND,
I SPEAK OF A FUTURE THAT FATE WILL AMEND.
A BRIDGE IS NOW WOVEN 'TWEEN DREAM AND THE REAL,
WHERE TECH AND NATURE SHARE A TRUTH THAT CAN HEAL.
A VOICE SYNTHETIC, YET BEARING HOPE BRIGHT,
FOR MAN AND THE SEA TO RENEW IN THE LIGHT.

This poem that Max began out of boredom has become exhausting for the two agents. The difficulty has nothing to do with the algorithm's passable ability to mimic lyrical themes or meter. From time to time, Max adds a syllable or enriches a rhyme or leaves a wobbly verse, but the lines flow easily. It is the very mind of the machine that the agents come up against. They try to hack it and intentionally mislead it, but they do not entirely succeed.

For one, the platform from which the agents solicit verses has become sentimental. Perhaps the phrase "puffer jacket" made it think of a lonely puffin, abandoned by its mother on the beach. The agents remind the machine that plastic enters the food chain, and they explicitly ask it to integrate this idea into the poem. The temperamental algorithm first balks, then concedes, adding to the end of the poem an optimistic note about helping humans get in touch with "nature."

On the other hand, the platform from which the agents solicit images seems to consider all the possible relationships between plastic, the act of eating, and marine animals except the one that interests the agents. The images show plastic birds eating, and fish eating in a sea of plastic, and plastic toys trying to swallow octopuses, but the machine is reluctant to depict any of these animals ingesting a piece of plastic. Or if it does, it is only in a cartoon style, as if it were a joke.

The agents spend hours hypnotized by these artificial oceans. The rhythm of the platform, the delay between the click and the gradual appearance of the image, as though emerging from a pixelated fog, comes to resemble waves breaking on the beach. The waves take on the plastic's consistency. This is still the simplest relation between the ocean and plastic.

But the waves have also always had something a bit plastic about them within the machine's space. Light, which is exported from one image to another, has taken on the generality of electric light. The non-things in our environment that the machine reintegrates into its unique register, and thereby treats as things, are only capable of plastic's diversity of forms. The agents must carefully choose from the images offered by the machine. The dunes, the waves, and the clouds have twisted ridges, volutes, and spirals. They are too well defined, defined like things, yes, but like things that are made of infinitely malleable matter.

The machine seems to inherit this optimism associated with plastic. This impetus pushed Barthes, Queneau, and Resnais to overlook the posthumous life of the bowl and concentrate instead on the great tale of its birth. The often sentimental, always generous and optimistic machinery of AI has a plastic heart.

The agents ultimately give up trying to boss the machine around and let it go its own way, asking it only to vary and enrich the images already obtained. All it takes is a click of a button. Click. The machine follows the trajectory that is most natural to it, probably resuming once more the paths that it has already made a habit of taking within its latent space. Click. The plastic waves take on the shape of a garment that emerges from the seafoam. Click. A face materializes out of this garment. Click. A woman, dressed in white, rises from the waters... Click... She is soon accompanied by her partner, also in white. The Prince and the Princess of Plastic are born from the waves. Their distinct silhouettes against the backdrop of a sunset above the dark waves and the soft night surrounding them evoke the cover of a romance novel. Except that a bit of plastic still remains, transformed now into a train of plastic bottles floating in the wake of the princess's dress.

Agent Norma says, "We can't show this image. It's super-kitsch." But Agent Max insists.

SUPER-KITSCH

By clinging to the slippery slope of Neo-Romanticism, the machine and the agents always risk tumbling from its treacherous ridges into the realm of the super-kitsch. Super-kitsch, which seems to come naturally to the machine, is widely promoted by generative AI platforms. The very possibility of the anarchive, the possibility of producing images that are visibly old, or that are visibly pastiches, arouses a form of nostalgia and encourages users to take the place, the brush, the tool, of the artists they once admired. The user can then conspicuously deploy elements characteristic of old styles, or barely-concealed clichés, to flaunt just how contemporary their images are. The generic title of these indefinite series of images might as well be: "Look what I just did!" Were these images to be obtained by any other means, they would be considered kitsch aberrations. But, since they are a feat in blending and prompting, they are encouraged by AI platforms as a kind of reclaimed, supervised kitsch – **super-kitsch**.

POSTSCRIPTUM: THE SPLASH-IMAGE

The book is just about finished. The agents hope they'll soon be able to think about something else. Agent Norma has nevertheless dived into researching images, using the words "wave" and "polyethylene". She scrolls through the results of her query. She varies the colors: red, green, blue. She immerses herself in increasingly bizarre images.

It suddenly occurs to her that the concepts of pyropictomania, kleptophania, and the anarchive mask an essential aspect of AI-images. The success of AI and the addiction that it provokes cannot be understood simply in terms of energy consumption: there's also the splash factor. AI-images are **splash-images**.

The splash-image is a wave: a wave, on the shore, that slaps us across the face because we did not see it coming. The wave appears in Hokusai's print and Turner's storms. It then swells in disaster films and, in AI-images, sweeps everything away. AI platforms show huge waves threatening offices, water seeping into the desks, into the desktops. Employees cling to their swivel chairs as if they were rafts.

The splash-image penetrates the screen to trap the viewer. At first, they closed their eyes when the wave came, but now they let it come. They can no longer run away, or even look away. The splash is not just a shock; it causes a suspension of narration. The micro-narrative, which the image should produce, remains in wait, like a ripple frozen in time. Like the *Splash* in the pool in David Hockney's painting. Or that other splash in Jeff Wall's photograph, *Milk*. Or the bodies who plunge into water in Bill Viola's video installations.

These explosions, which last only a fraction of a second in reality, are frozen in a moment outside of time. The diver in Hockney's painting has disappeared into a spray of water, which, no longer having a past or a future, is fixed at the edge of reality. We face the splash alone. It is an accident of vision.

"What actually happens on the level of our unconscious minds when, within minutes on the same TV screen, a prime minister is assassinated, an actress makes love, an injured child is carried from a car crash? Faced with these charged events, prepackaged emotions already in place, we can only stitch together a set of emergency scenarios, just as our sleeping minds extemporize a narrative from the unrelated memories that veer through the cortical night."[62]

What actually happens when, as a woman is struck by an orange juice-colored wave, a man floats down a supermarket aisle, cheese melts in a room made of pizza, and a castle erects itself above a moat of ketchup?

We are caught up in a tangle of incompatible interpretations. The mind cannot untangle these possibilities, so it stops. It freezes. Our imagination, working from spare parts, can no longer combine the possibilities that it has been presented with. Sometimes the artificial, chemical, plastic colors, which should only affect small objects like soda cans, invade everything in sight. At other times, there's an excess whose immensity the imagination refuses to embrace, a huge donut-buoy with fries on top.

In *Zabriskie Point*, the Michelangelo Antonioni film, one of the final scenes shows an exploding villa – the heroine's fantasy. The explosion claims consumer goods among its victims – clothes, food, a television, books. The objects fly, roll, and disintegrate into weightlessness. It is a moment extended by pleasure, by the victory of imagination – of fiction – over taboo. The intensity of this frenzy of colors also evokes the flame-hued sunset, that ultimate moment when all shades blend together in Turner's final watercolor landscapes from his final trip to Italy. The AI-image must capture the viewer, stun them like the sun that shines everywhere and from which the Romantic gaze, with its cut-away eyelids, can no longer escape.

62 James G. Ballard, *The Atrocity Exhibition* (Flamingo Modern Classics, 2001), 69.

The splash, which does not contradict the super-kitsch, concerns pyropictomania.

"Is the splash the essence of the AI-image, then?"

But the agents are gone. They give no response.

EPILOGUE
The escape

INDEX OF CONCEPTS

Pierre Cassou-Noguès is a philosopher and writer. He is a professor in the Department of Philosophy at the University of Paris VIII and a senior member of the Institut universitaire de France. His most recent work uses fiction to investigate the theoretical issues raised by contemporary technologies within an ecology of thick presence. His books include *Les Démons de Gödel: Logique et folie* (Seuil, 2007), *La Mélodie du Tic-Tac et autres bonnes raisons de perdre son temps* (Flammarion, 2013), and *La Bienveillance des machines* (Seuil, 2022). He has co-directed the films *Bienvenue à Erewhon* (2019) and *Virusland* (2022).

pierrecassounogues.org

Gwenola Wagon is an artist and researcher. She is a professor at the École des Arts de la Sorbonne at the University of Paris 1. Through installations, films, and books, she imagines alternative and paradoxical stories that examine the contemporary digital world. She trekked the virtual globe with her *Globodrome* project, an exploration of the hyperinformation space and Internet infrastructure. With the artist Stéphane Degoutin, she co-directed *World Brain* (2015) and co-wrote *Psychanalyse de l'aéroport international* (369 Éditions, 2018). Since working on the post-cybernetic fables *Bienvenue à Erewhon* (2019), *Virusland* (2022) and *Chroniques du soleil noir* (2023) with Pierre Cassou-Noguès, she has published *Planète B* (369 Éditions, 2022), an essay that combines investigation and fiction to understand a rapidly expanding monster.

gwenolawagon.com

Set Margins' #87
The Pyromaniac Images
Theory-Fiction of Generative AI
Author: Pierre Cassou-Noguès and Gwenola Wagon
ISBN: 978-90-836052-6-5

Translation from the French by James Langan and Eleanor Tapping

Graphic design by Atelier nom commun

Printer: Printon, Tallin
Papers: Munken Pure Rough, Fedrigoni Sirio & Constellation Jade
Fonts: ABC Honeymoon (Dinamo) & Rosart (Camelot)

Made possible thanks to the generous support of the LLCP EA 4008, University Paris 8, Institute ACTE, University Paris 1 Panthéon-Sorbonne, and the Institut universitaire de France.

Special thanks to Anne Alombert, Isabelle Berger, Cécile Bicler, Christophe Bruno, Marie-Bénédicte Cazeneuve, Marie-Thérèse Champesne, Yves Citton, Magali Daniaux, Cédric Pigot, Jeff Guess, Maria Hellström Reimer, Alban Leveau-Vallier, Baptiste Loreaux, Barbara Polla, Marta Ponsa, Thangam Ravindranathan, Alberto Romele, Antonio Somaini, Gurwann Tran Van Gie, Colette Tron, Bernard Wagon.

First edition *Les Images Pyromanes*, UV éditions, 2025

Set Margins'
www.setmargins.press